Science for Development of Super Mature Society

— Cultivate global human resource who will lead super mature society

超成熟社会発展のサイエンス

── 超成熟社会をリードするグローバル博士人材の育成

Keio Leading Graduate School Program
慶應義塾大学博士課程教育リーディングプログラム編

慶應義塾大学出版会

International President Forum, March 3, 2015, Keio University
From the right side toward the left side: Prof. Makabe, Prof. Petrović, Prof. Hamada, Prof. Seike, Prof. Tan, Ms. Beale, Prof. Poitou, Prof. Kannari.

Science for Development of Super Mature Society
— Cultivate global human resource who will lead super mature society

超成熟社会発展のサイエンス
――超成熟社会をリードするグローバル博士人材の育成

KEIO UNIVERSITY PRESS, Tokyo
慶應義塾大学出版会, 東京

Preface

Professor Atsushi Seike
President, Keio University

We are currently living in a time of great changes. Declining birthrates and ageing population, global warming, intensification of regional conflicts, and increasingly fierce competition in the global market—these are all drastic structural changes that challenge the very sustainability of our society. We believe that these are typical issues of a super-mature society.

Scientific insight is indispensable to solving these issues. This requires deeper research within the disciplines while promoting an interdisciplinary approach that applies these research results across the different academic fields. Researchers and specialists are expected to have high-level research and analytical skills within their field and to have the ability to generate holistic solutions by understanding the developments within other disciplines and establishing close communication between them. In this respect, graduate schools thus far have devoted to conducting education and research that places value on making academic contributions and have been producing doctorate holders that go on to pursue careers teaching at universities or as researchers. However, in order to cope with the difficult challenges of a super-mature society head-on, society now calls for a new type of doctorate holder who can demonstrate both creative planning and high management skills in a broader range of areas, from policy making at the national and regional levels to playing key roles in new business innovation. In contrast to the increasing number of students obtaining doctorates in the United States, China, UK, and Korea, the number is decreasing slightly in Japan, but we may be able to reverse this trend if we meet the need for nurturing this new type of doctorate holder.

This program, "Science for the Development of a Super Mature Society"—which aims to foster the next generation of capable

はじめに

清家　篤（慶應義塾長）

　今日私たちの社会は大きな構造変化の時代をむかえています。それは、少子高齢化、地球温暖化、地域紛争の深刻化、グローバルな市場競争の激化といった、社会の持続可能性そのものを問うような変化です。それは超成熟社会の問題と言うこともできます。

　それらの問題の解決には科学的な洞察が不可欠であり、それは個別分野の研究を一層深めると同時に、それぞれの研究分野の成果を横断的に活用する学際的な取り組みが必要となります。研究者や専門家には専門分野での高い研究・分析能力と、他分野の発展を理解し、分野間で密接なコミュニケーションをとりながら総合的な解決策を生み出す能力が求められているのです。この点でこれまでの大学院では専ら学術的貢献に価値をおく教育研究活動が中心であり、教員や研究者になる博士が輩出されてきましたが、今後は、これまでの博士と異なる新しい職域として、国や地方の政策決定や、産業界の新規事業部門の場等で、独創的な企画力と高いマネージメント力を駆使して超成熟社会の難問に立ち向かっていく、新しい型の博士も必要になってきます。世界の博士号取得者の数は、米国、中国、イギリス、韓国で増加傾向にあるのに対し、日本はやや減少傾向にありますが、上述のタイプの博士育成のニーズに応えることで、博士号取得者減少の反転にも繋がります。

　このような次代の博士を育成すべく、本プログラムは、本格的な文理融合と産業界・行政との密な連携による革新的とも言える教育システムを備え、平成23年度に文部科学省の博士課程教育リーディングプログラムに採択され、24年度から1期生を採用し、すでに4年目になりました。この間、学内の協力に加え、産業界や政府・自治体から賜りましたご理解ご支援に、改めて深く感謝申し上げます。本プログラムは5年一貫の教育システムであり、まもなく1期生が社会に輩出されるこの時期に、

doctorate holders and is based on an innovative educational system that integrates the humanities and sciences and promotes close collaboration with government and industry—was selected in 2011 for the Program for Leading Graduate Schools of the Ministry of Education, Culture, Sports, Science and Technology. The first students entered the program in 2012, and now the program is in its fourth year. I would like to take this opportunity to again thank the university, the business community, and national and local governments for their immense support. The curriculum spans five years, and this publication was planned just as we are about to send off our first cohort into society.

The part 1 introduces the content of the discussions at the International Presidents Forum held in March this year, to which the presidents of five world-leading universities contributed. The talks centered on how universities should respond to these new changes taking place in the global society. The chapter 1 of the part 2 is a re-edit of the prefaces for the program's newsletters, which includes opinions of leaders in various sectors of society. The chapter 2 of the part 2 describes the structure of the program and the current status of its initiatives.

By taking on responsibilities in various new fields, next-generation doctorate holders may experience a great number of difficulties until they establish themselves in society. I hope that our doctoral students, to whom we are devoting a great deal of effort to training and nurturing as part of our graduate school reforms, will find their place in society where they can play an active role and contribute to the building of an affluent economy and society.

Lastly, I hope that you all continue to lend us your warm support and guidance for the program in the years to come.

本出版は企画されました。

　第1部では、このような新しい変化に対応する大学のあり方について、世界の5大学の学長の参加を得て本年3月に開催したフォーラムでの討論内容を掲載しました。そして第2部では、その1章に本プログラムの機関紙であるNewsletterの巻頭言を再編集し、各界のリーダーからのご意見を掲載しました。引き続く2章では、本プログラムの仕組みと取り組み状況について、ご説明いたしました。

　次代の博士は、新しい職域を担うことになるがゆえに、その社会に出た後の定着までは幾多の困難もあろうかと思います。大学院改革の一環として手塩にかけて育成した新しい時代の博士たちにどうか活躍の機会をお与え頂き、これが豊かな社会・経済の構築の一助となれますよう祈念しております。

　最後に私どものこのプログラムに対して、各方面の皆様方から今後ともこれまでに変わらぬご支援とご鞭撻を賜りますよう、改めてお願い申し上げます。

Contents

Preface
Professor Atsushi Seike, President, Keio University 2

Part 1 International Presidents Forum
Presidents of five eminent universities discuss
—Cultivate human resource who will lead
the revolutionary times— 15

Prologue
Toshiaki Makabe, Vice President of Keio University 24

Chapter 1
**Present status of five universities through number,
and recent trend** 28

1.1 The University of Tokyo 28
1.2 University of Oxford 38
1.3 Ecole Centrale Nantes 44
1.4 National University of Singapore 56
1.5 Keio University 64

Chapter 2
Future prospects for education and research of university
—**Discuss a lot of tradeoff issues**— 72

Closing 98

目次

はじめに
清家 篤（慶應義塾長）3

第 1 部 国際学長フォーラム
世界の 5 大学学長が討論
—大変革の時代を担う人材の育成— 15

はじめに
真壁利明（慶應義塾 常任理事）25

第 1 章
数字で見る 5 大学の現状と最近の動き 29

1.1 東京大学 29
1.2 オックスフォード大学 39
1.3 エコール サントラル ナント校 45
1.4 シンガポール国立大学 57
1.5 慶應義塾大学 65

第 2 章
大学の教育と研究の将来展望
—多くのトレードオフ問題を議論する— 73

終わりに 99

Part 2
Keio, Five-year Program for Leading Graduate School 103

Chapter 1
Essays Presented by Leaders 104

1. OPENING OF KEIO'S PROGRAM
1.1 On the launch of the Science for Development of Super Mature Society Program **Atsushi Seike** 104
1.2 Basic Philosophy Guiding the Science Program for Development of Super Mature Society **Kouhei Ohnishi** 108
1.3 Close Encounters of the Third Kind **Akira Haseyama** 112

2. ANTICIPATION OF KEIO'S PROGRAM
2.1 A Bridgehead for a New 'Encouragement of Learning' **Kan Suzuki** 118
2.2 Great Expectations for Keio's New Program **Roger Goodman** 122
2.3 Great Hopes in Keio's Challenge: Development Global Leaders from Japan **Takashi Kawamura** 128
2.4 Learn in Both Eastern and Western Ways **Ichiro Fujisaki** 132
2.5 Adaptability, Entrepreneurial Spirit and the Ability To Meet Challenges at the Interface of Multiple Domains: Here are Educational Objectives of the Keio University Program of Excellence **Arnaud Poitou** 136
2.6 Expectation of the Keio Program for Leading Graduate School **Hideo Aiso** 140
2.7 Expectations for Leader Development in the Program for Leading Graduate School **Hirotsune Satoh** 144

第2部
慶應義塾、5年一貫リーディング大学院プログラム　　　103

第1章
リーディング大学院プログラムに寄せて　　　105

1. プログラム開設にあたって

1.1 超成熟社会発展のサイエンスプログラムの開始にあたって
　清家 篤　105
1.2 超成熟社会発展のサイエンスプログラムの基本方針
　大西公平　109
1.3 「未知との遭遇」がはじまった？
　長谷山 彰　113

2. プログラムへの期待

2.1 新たな「学問のすゝめ」の橋頭保に
　鈴木 寛　119
2.2 慶應の新プログラムに対する Oxford からの期待
　Roger Goodman　123
2.3 慶應義塾のチャレンジ，「グローバルリーダー育成」に期待して
　川村 隆　129
2.4 日米双方のメリットを活かす
　藤崎一郎　133
2.5 適応力・起業家精神・そして多彩な分野におけるチャレンジを支援する慶應義塾大学リーディングプログラムの教育目標
　Arnaud Poitou　137
2.6 慶應義塾大学リーディングプログラムへの期待
　相磯秀夫　141
2.7 リーディング大学院プログラムにおけるリーダー育成へ産業界から期待する
　佐藤博恒　145

2.8 Some thoughts of the Keio Program for Leading Graduate School **Norihiko Fukuda** 148

2.9 A Great Hope for the Keio Leading Graduate School Program: To Cultivate Graduate Students to Have Dreams and Achieve Them **Hiroshi Nagano** 152

2.10 To Demonstrate the Vitality of Japan's "Super Mature Society" at the 2020 Olympic and Paralympic Games in Tokyo to World **Mutsuko Hatano** 156

3. EXPECTATION FOR HIGH-LEVEL Ph.D. IN GLOVAL SOCIETY

3.1 The Third Opening of Japan and High-level Postgraduate Human Resource Development **Toshiaki Makabe** 160

3.2 The War for Talent Continues **Yumiko Murakami** 168

3.3 Innovative Doctoral Training **Kurt Deketelaere** 172

3.4 Japan's Economy on Track by Creating New Markets with Innovation and Converting the Industrial Structure **Yoshihiko Nagasato** 176

3.5 Leaders with Integrated Expertise in Both Natural and Social Sciences in Developing Super Mature Society **Yoshio Higuchi** 180

3.6 Expectations for Leaders **Atsushi Miura** 188

3.7 Development of Global Mindest, Skill and Leadership **Tojiro Aoyama** 192

3.8 To The Keio Program for Leading Graduate School **Takemitsu Kunio** 196

3.9 Never Give Up **Ryo Kubota** 200

3.10 Expectation for High-level Ph.Ds. **Kaoru Kuzume** 204

3.11 Leadership Aptitude: Is it Inherent or Acquired ? **Fumihiko Kannari** 208

2.8 慶應義塾リーディング大学院プログラムによせて
　　福田紀彦 149
2.9 夢を描き行動にうつせる人材を育むリーディング大学院に
　　永野 博 153
2.10 東京オリンピック・パラリンピック 2020 で「超成熟社会」の活力を世界に披露
　　波多野 睦子 157

3. 高度博士人材への期待
3.1 第三の開国と大学院高度博士人材育成
　　真壁利明 161
3.2 トップ国際人材の獲得競争は続く
　　村上由美子 169
3.3 想像力に富んだ博士の養成
　　Kurt Deketelaere 173
3.4 イノベーションにより新市場を創生し、産業構造を転換して日本経済を成長軌道にのせよう
　　永里善彦 177
3.5 超成熟社会発展に求められる文理融合リーダー
　　樋口美雄 181
3.6 川崎市が期待するリーダー像
　　三浦 淳 189
3.7 豊かな国際力の育成
　　青山藤詞郎 193
3.8 生産性高い議論の場から育つ博士人材に期待して
　　國尾武光 197
3.9 あきらめないこと
　　窪田 良 201
3.10 リーディング学生への期待
　　葛目 薫 205
3.11 先天的か後天的か：リーダーの資質
　　神成文彦 209

Chapter 2
Program for Leading Graduate School (PLGS):
Framework and Current Status 212

Introduction
Fumihiko Kannari 212

1. Goal and program 216
2. Program Outline 218
3. Educational system (MMD system realizes genuine integration of arts and sciences) 224
4. Program curriculum 232
5. Cultivating human resources through the collaboration with industry and government (Group project exercise) 242
6. Cultivating a broad perspective of view and vision through designing of three pillars 244
7. Diverse activities that increase motivation (Overseas dispatch, summer/winter camps, etc.) 246
8. e-learning Cloud system connecting campuses 254
9. Members 258

Editorial Note
Toshiaki Makabe 268

第 2 章
リーディング大学院プログラム—その仕組みと取組状況—　　213

はじめに
神成文彦　213

1. プログラムの目的　217
2. プログラムの特長　219
3. 教育システム（MMD システムによる本格的な文理融合の実現）　225
4. プログラム設置科目　233
5. 産業界・行政体との密な連携による人材育成
   （グループプロジェクト演習）　243
6. 三位一体設計による人間力形成
   （主専攻 / 副専攻 / グループプロジェクト演習）　245
7. モチベーションを高める多様な活動
   （海外派遣、夏・冬キャンプ、e.t.c.）　247
8. 他キャンパスを繋ぐ e- ラーニングクラウドシステム　255
9. メンバー構成　259

編集後記
真壁利明（慶應義塾大学リーディング大学院プログラム ボード会議議長）　269

Part 1　第1部

International Presidents Forum
国際学長フォーラム

Presidents of five eminent universities discuss
—Cultivate human resource who will lead
the revolutionary times—

世界の5大学学長が討論
—大変革の時代を担う人材の育成—

Main speaker
Atsushi SEIKE
清家　篤

Atsushi SEIKE is President of Keio University since 2009. Received a PhD in Labor Economics from Keio University in 1993. Became a Professor at Keio's Faculty of Business and Commerce in 1992 and served as Dean from 2007-9. Was a Visiting Scholar at UCLA, Consultant at RAND Corporation, and Visiting Principal Research Officer at the Economic Research Institute, Economic Planning Agency. Specialist in Labor Economics, authoring many articles and books on the labor market and ageing population. Currently, Chairman of the Council for Promotion of Social Security System Reform; member of the Industrial Structure Council and Chairman of its Manufacturing Industry Committee; member of the WEF Global University Leaders Forum and WEF Global Agenda Council on Ageing. President of the Japan Association of Private Universities and Colleges since March, 2011 and President of. The Japan Society of Human Resource Management since September 2015.

慶應義塾長。慶應義塾大学商学部教授。博士（商学）、専攻は労働経済学。1992年慶應義塾大学商学部教授、2007年同商学部長を経て2009年慶應義塾長就任。現在、社会保障制度改革推進会議議長、日本私立大学連盟会長、日本労務学会会長、World Economic Forum Global Agenda Council on Ageing メンバーなどを兼務。

Main speaker
Junichi HAMADA
濱田純一

Junichi HAMADA has served as the 29th President of the University of Tokyo until March 2015 and is now Professor Emeritus. During the 6-year term of presidency, he embarked on a series of progressive reforms on the University's educational system, aspiring to educate students to become "More Tough, Global, and Resilient". He received his Bachelor's, Master's, and PhD degrees in law from the University of Tokyo. His academic interest lies in the freedom of expression, and of the press and broadcasting media in the Information Society. He started his academic career at the University of Tokyo as a research associate in 1978, promoted to the Professor of Information Law and Policy in 1992, and served as the Director of the Institute of Socio-Information and Communication Studies in 1994. His long-lasting endeavor to accelerate the University's educational reforms became prominent in 1999, when he contributed to establishing a new Graduate School of Interdisciplinary Information Studies and served as the first Dean.

東京大学総長。東京大学教授を経て現在同大学名誉教授。法学博士。1992年東京大学教授、同大学社会情報研究所所長、同大学大学院学際情報学府長（初代）などを経て、2009年から2015年3月まで第29代東京大学総長。東京大学で学士、修士、博士の学位を得る。専門は情報化社会の表現の自由、報道や放送メディアの自由論。

Main speaker
Alison BEALE
アリソン ビール

Alison BEALE is Director of the University of Oxford Japan Office, a post she has held since September 2012. Before that she was a long-serving staff member of the British Council holding senior posts in Japan, Trinidad and Tobago, Shanghai, and most recently Tokyo where she was Deputy Director Japan from 2009 - 2012. In this post she had particular responsibility for Higher Education projects, focussing on collaboration and knowledge transfer, skills development for PhD students, student and staff mobility and alumni relations for strategic planning and partnership development. She has a career specialising in Japan spanning 15 years and first came to the country on the JET Programme in 1993 when she was based in Oita Prefecture.

オックスフォード大学日本事務所代表（2012年）。オックスフォード大学卒業。シェフィールド大学大学院修士（日本研究）。JETプログラムで初来日し、大分県で英語指導を行う。15年間にわたって日本で国際交流や文化交流に従事し、中国、トリニダード・トバゴ、日本でブリティッシュ・カウンシルの管理職を歴任。2009年から2012年まで日本のブリティッシュ・カウンシルで副代表を務め、主に日本の高等教育機関との連携構築・強化に従事。

Main speaker
Arnaud POITOU
アルノー ポワトー

Arnaud POITOU is Director of Ecole Centrale de Nantes since 2012. He received his engineering degree at Ecole Polytechnique, and his Ph.D. degree at Ecole des Mines de Paris in 1987. He became a Professor of Mechanical Engineering at Ecole Normale Supérieure de Cachan in 1995 and then moved to Ecole Centrale de Nantes in 2002. His main research activities concerned materials processing with a special emphasis on composite forming. Within this framework he developed important links with industries including aeronautics (Airbus, Daher, Stelia, …) and automotive companies (Renault Nissan, Faurecia, Valeo …). He served as a guest professor at Ecole Polytechnique.

エコール サントラル ナント校長。エコール サントラル（EC）ナント教授。エコール ポリテクニーク（パリ）卒業後、パリ国立高等鉱業学校修了。工学博士。1995 年 ENS Cachan 機械工学科教授、2002 年 EC ナント教授をへて 2012 年 EC ナント校長就任。エコール ポリテクニークの客員教授。専門は複合材料プロセス。航空機や自動車産業との産学連携に貢献。

Main speaker
Chorh Chuan TAN
チョウ チョア タン

Chorh Chuan TAN is President of the National University of Singapore since 2008. He graduated from the National University of Singapore (NUS) in 1983. He became a Professor of Medicine at NUS since 1999. He was Dean of the Faculty of Medicine from 1997 to 2000. He served as the NUS's Provost and Deputy President between 2004 and 2007. He concurrently serves as the Chairman of the Board of the National University Health System, Deputy Chairman of Singapore's Agency for Science, Technology and Research, and Director of Monetary Authority of Singapore. He is the Chair of the World Economic Forum's Global University Leaders Forum and a member of the Forum's Global Agenda Council on the Future of Jobs. He is a Fellow of the Royal College of Physicians of London and of Edinburgh, American College of Physicians and Royal Geographical Society, UK.

シンガポール国立大学 (NUS) 学長。NUS 医学部教授。1997 年同大学医学部長、2004 年同大学学長代理をへて 2008 年 NUS 学長就任。現在、シンガポール国立大学ヘルスシステム会長、シンガポール科学技術研究庁の副議長、シンガポール通貨金融庁所長、世界経済フォーラムのグローバル大学リーダーフォーラム議長などを務める。ロイヤルカレッジ内科学会 (ロンドン・エジンバラ)、米国内科学会、王立地理学会の各フェロー。

Commentator
Zoran PETROVIĆ
ゾラン ペトロビッチ

Zoran PETROVIĆ is a member of Serbian Academy of Sciences and Arts, and the Secretary of the Department of Applied Physics. He obtained his B.Eng. and M.Sc. degrees at University of Belgrade and his Ph.D. thesis at the Australian National University (Canberra) in 1985. He is a Professor and Director of COE for non-equilibrium processes at the Institute of Physics, Belgrade. He served as a Professor at University of Belgrade as well as a visiting professor at Keio University. He has been vice president of the National Council for Science and Technology of Serbia, and is a Fellow of American Physical Society. He has won Marko Jaric Award for his "great contribution to low temperature plasma kinetics and diagnostics and to atomic and molecular collision physics."

セルビア科学芸術アカデミー会員・同応用物理部門幹事。ベオグラード物理研究所教授。理学博士。1978年ベオグラード大学電気工学科卒業、1980年同大学応用物理専攻修士、1985年オーストラリア国立大学博士課程修了。ベオグラード大学教授を兼担。慶應義塾大学訪問教授やセルビア科学技術会議の副会長などを務める。原子分子物理や低温プラズマ運動論への貢献で Marko Jaric Award を受賞。APS（米国）フェロー。専門は低温プラズマの素過程など。

Organizer
Toshiaki MAKABE
真壁利明

Toshiaki MAKABE is the Vice-President of Keio University in charge of research since 2009. He received his BSc, MSc, and PhD degrees all from Keio University. He became a Professor of Electrical Engineering at Keio University in 1991. He served as a guest professor at POSTECH, Ruhr University Bochum, and Xi'an Jiaotong University. He was Dean of the Faculty of Science and Technology from 2007. He has authored many books, including *Plasma Electronics: Applications in Microelectronic Device Fabrication* (2nd-edition) published by CRC in 2014. He received the awards "Fluid Science Prize"(2003) from Tohoku University; "Plasma Electronics Prize"(2004) from the JSAP; and the "Plasma Prize"(2006) from the American Vacuum Society. He is an elected fellow of the Institute of Physics (UK), the AVS (US), the JSAP, and the Japan Federation of Engineering Societies for his *"Pioneering contributions to modeling and design of low temperature plasma and surface processes."*

慶應義塾常任理事。同大学理工学部名誉教授。工学博士。1991年同大学理工学部教授、2007年理工学部長をへて2009年常任理事就任。ポハン工科大学、ルール大学ボッフム、西安交通大学の各客員教授。著書「PLASMA ELECTRONICS」(2nd-Edn; CRC 2014) 他多数。低温プラズマと表面プロセスの研究で、「流体科学賞」(東北大)、「プラズマエレクトロニクス賞」(応物学会)、「プラズマ賞」(米国AVS) を受賞。IOP (英国)、AVS (米国)、JSAP (日本)、JFES (日本) の各フェロー。

Facilitator
Fumihiko KANNARI
神成文彦

Fumihiko KANNARI is a Chief Professor in charge of education in the Graduate School of Science and Technologies, Keio University since 2008. He serves as a Coordinator of All-Round Program for Leading Graduate School (PLGS), supported by MEXT, "Science for Development of Super Mature Society" of Keio University since 2013. He received the B.S., M.S., and Ph.D. degrees in Electrical Engineering from Keio University in 1980, 1882, and 1985, respectively. In 1984 he was a Research Associate at SERC Rutherford Appleton Laboratory. In 1986 he joined Spectra Technology, Inc., Bellevue, WA as a Senior Scientist. In 1988 he joined Keio University, where he is currently a Professor in the Department of Electronics and Electrical Engineering. He was a Keio Fellow at Downing College, Cambridge University in 2000. He has published more than 200 international papers in refereed journals in the field of laser physics and quantum electronics.

慶應義塾大学理工学研究科学習指導主任。同大学電子工学科教授。工学博士。2013年リーディング大学院プログラム(オールラウンド型)、"超成熟社会発展のサイエンス" コーディネータ。1980年慶應義塾大学工学部卒業、同大学工学研究科電気工学専攻修士、博士課程電気工学専攻修了。1984年 SERC Rutherford Appleton Laboratory ポスドク研究員、1986年 Spectra Technology 社上級研究員を経て、1988年慶應義塾大学理工学部に奉職。2000年 Cambridge 大学 Downing 校 Keio Fellow。専門はレーザー工学・光量子エレクトロニクス。

Prologue

Toshiaki Makabe, Vice President of Keio University
Let me introduce you to the purpose of this forum. The main title of the present forum is 'Science to Strengthen a Super-Mature Society', of course. This year is the 70th anniversary from the end of the World War II. The period overlaps the history of the invention of the transistor and the successive progress of LSIs. The development of microelectronics has made a society of information, communication technology and produced a global society. In such a global society, information can be instantly shared. Now, the geopolitical situations have been drastically changed. On the other hand, the rapid development of the economy has brought various problems such as global warming, ozone destruction and so on. We are now facing the great challenge of the sustainability of Spaceship Earth. At the same time in Japan, we intend to develop our super-mature society from the aging society with a low birthrate after an economy has passed its peak.

When we re-design a modern society at present, we can get clues to solving complicated and difficult problems which often demand compromises by using policy studies as well as pure sciences cooperatively, and such a way should bring us to the global standard. Unfortunately, we have no existing example of advanced nation with a super-mature society. Therefore, Japan has to make a solitary start domestically and internationally for a renewed civilization and further industrial development.

At all times, society has been counting on universities a lot. Now, the high- level development of human resources which is an original mission of university, is an urgent issue and society is eagerly expecting the universities to solve it. In particular in Japan, it is necessary to act and renovate the framework of education and research. Our previous passive education system with overemphasis on knowledge should be renovated to an active one

はじめに

真壁利明（慶應義塾 常任理事）

　本フォーラムの目的を私からご紹介します。フォーラムのテーマは「超成熟社会発展のためのサイエンス」です。今年は第二次世界大戦の終結から70年を迎えます。この年月はトランジスタの発明に端を発したLSI（集積回路）の進化の歴史とも重なります。マイクロエレクトロニクスの発展はICT（情報通信技術）社会をもたらし、グローバル社会を生み出しました。世界中で瞬時に情報が共有されるグローバル社会の下で、その地政学的状況は70年前に比べて著しく変化しています。他方で、急速な経済成長は地球温暖化やオゾン層破壊など、さまざまな問題を引き起こしています。我々はいま、宇宙船地球号の持続可能性という極めて困難な課題に直面しています。同時に、日本では高度経済成長が終焉したあとの少子高齢化社会の到来に伴い、超成熟社会への発展を目指す時機でもあります。

　新しい社会を再設計するとき、しばしばトレードオフの選択が求められる複雑で困難な課題に出会います。その際、専門分野の科学と技術が政策の科学と連携して取り組むなかから解決の糸口は見出されるでしょう。このようなアプローチを通して我々はグローバルスタンダードへと到達するはずです。超成熟社会に突入した先進国がないなかで、この文明のレノベーションと産業の更なる高度化に向け日本は単独で歩み始めなければなりません。

　いつの時代も大学は社会から頼られてきました。高度人材の育成が大学本来の使命であることは論を待ちませんが、いま超成熟社会を発展させることが喫緊の課題であり、大学に寄せられる期待には極めて大きいものがあります。現在、日本では教育と研究の枠組のレノベーションに迫

which makes students develop the ability to find clues to solving various problems by thinking and judging for themselves and making rational presentations. This is a need of the times. We believe the key for the development of the super-mature and aging society with a low birthrate is to nurture and launch talented fresh Ph.D. who possesses the skill for drawing from and presenting the overview of efforts to be made when they face a complicated and entangled issue.

At Keio University, a 5-year program 'Science to Strengthen a Super-Mature Society' for masters to doctors' course has been established in the campus free from any constraint due to geopolitical influence. For the sake of the students who have been selected for the program by competition, we arrange a team consisting of the supervisor in their faculty and qualified supportive vice-supervisors from enterprises, other faculties, overseas universities, and senior mentors from industry and government.

During the process of transition to a small but prosperous mature society with people's satisfaction, the system which was established at the time of the booming economy should certainly be reformed, and academia cannot be indifferent to such a reform. The UK, France and Singapore as well as Japan all will approach the coming super-mature society with a different system and policy in synchronized with their respective higher education and research in academia.

Under these circumstances and this understanding, in the present International Presidents' Forum, we will have two round tables. One is the discussion on the present state of affairs, and the other is on how academia functions for countries, regions and transnational citizenship in future society. We very much expect deep discussion and thoughtful proposal to our near future global society from the present International Presidents' Forum. Thank you very much.

られています。従来の知識偏重で受動的な教育システムを、能動的なものへと刷新する必要があるでしょう。学生は能動的なシステムのもと自分自身で考え、判断し、論ずることで、さまざまな課題の解決へ向けその糸口を見出す能力を身に着けることです。これが時代の要請です。少子高齢化の下で超成熟社会へ発展するための鍵は、才能あふれる若き高度博士人材、すなわち複雑に絡み合った問題に接したときしかるべき取組の大筋を描き説明する技量を身に着けた人材、の育成と輩出にあると信じています。

慶應義塾大学は修士課程から博士課程までの5年一貫の大学院課程を対象とした「超成熟社会発展のサイエンス」と称するプログラムを、既存のキャンパスから独立した日吉西別館に2012年春に開設しています。このプログラムに競争的に選抜された大学院生のために、本人が所属する研究科の指導教員、他研究科や海外大学からの副指導教員、産業界や行政体から派遣されるシニアメンターがチーム、いわゆる「文理融合の水飲み場」を構成しています。

社会がその規模を縮小させつつあるなかで、人々が満足する豊かな成熟社会へと移行する過程では、経済が拡大している時代に構築されたシステムが変革を受けることは当然です。教育研究機関もこの変革に無関係でいることはできません。日本と同様、本日お迎えした各学長の母国、英国、フランス、シンガポールにおいても、それぞれの高等教育研究機関と連携・連動しながら来るべき超成熟社会に向け独自のシステムを構築し政策を講じてゆかれるでしょう。このような認識のもと、この国際学長フォーラムでは2つのセッションを設けています。第1章ではアカデミアばかりでなく国際社会を先導している各大学の現状に関する議論を、第2章では教育研究機関が今後の社会で国や地域や国境を越えて人々のつながりに果たす役割について議論を予定しています。この国際学長フォーラムでグローバル社会について深い議論が展開され、思慮に富んだ提案がなされることを期待しています。ありがとうございました。

Chapter 1
Present status of five universities through number, and recent trend

Fumihiko Kannari

Everybody knows what is the super-mature society. I think the mature society is a common word but if you pick the super but I find it might be combined mature society issue and aging issues, and then the social system becomes more complicated. There are many other issues, so we call the super-mature society. I would like to move on to the first session.

In the first session, we will discuss the present and near-future progress of each of universities. First I would like to ask you to present the status of your university including some numerical data, and if you have any ongoing project to develop or expand the higher education, please introduce these. May I ask Professor Hamada first?

1.1 The University of Tokyo ("U-Tokyo")
Junichi Hamada

Thank you, Professor Kannari. Professor Makabe has already talked about various issues of a super-mature society. I will not reiterate them. Instead, I would like to briefly address the issue of what and how we, in academia, can contribute to society at large today. Let me begin by showing you some notable characteristics and figures of the University of Tokyo. I hereafter say "U-Tokyo". Indeed, we often call our university "Todai", but

第1部　国際学長フォーラム

第1章
数字で見る5大学の現状と最近の動き

神成文彦

　　　　　　超成熟社会とは何かに関しては、皆様ご存じのとおりです。成熟社会という用語は一般的に用いられていると思いますが、そこに「超」を冠します。つまり成熟社会の問題と少子高齢化の問題を重ねると、社会システムはより複雑なものとなります。他にも多くの問題があります。それゆえ我々は超成熟社会と呼んでいるのです。さて、最初のセッションを始めましょう。

　第1セッションでは、まずご自身の大学の現状に関し数字を交えてお話いただき、教育促進を目的に進めているプロジェクトがあればご紹介いただきたいと思います。それでは濱田総長、お願いします。

1.1　東京大学
濱田純一

　　　　　　神成先生、ありがとうございました。超成熟社会の様々な問題についてはすでに真壁教授よりお話がありましたので、私から繰り返すことはいたしません。その代わりに、教育研究機関として我々大学が今日の社会全般に何を提供し、いかに貢献し得るかという問題に関して簡単に述べたいと思います。

　まず東京大学、これ以降はU-Tokyoと称しますが、U-Tokyoに関する顕著な特徴ならびに数字の説明から始めさせていた

it is rather difficult to be remembered in foreign countries, so we now use "U-Tokyo" as a popular name in English.

Our university is renowned as a comprehensive university which has 10 faculties, 15 graduate schools and 11 research institutes, covering almost all of the academic disciplines. We have about 14,000 undergraduate students and about 13,000 postgraduate students. The fact that U-Tokyo has the almost same number of undergraduates and postgraduates illustrates one of the characteristics of our university as a research-intensive university.

Our academic staff consists of 1300 tenured professors, 900 tenured associate professors, 100 non-tenured professors and 175 non-tenured associate professors. Non-tenured professors mostly belong to the faculties in the fields of natural science. In addition, we have a large number of non-tenured assistant professors of around 1400. This is another characteristic of a research-intensive university. Of all the tenured academic staff, those in the fields of humanities and social science account for about 19%.

[Appendix] The source of data is U-Tokyo Guide book in FY2013.
* Share of undergraduate students of each department:
  29% for Faculty of Engineering, 13% for Faculty of Law, 12% for Faculty of Letters, 9% for Faculty of Science, 7% for Faculty of Medicine, etc.
* Share of graduate students of each major:
  24% for Graduate School of Engineering, 10% for Graduate School of Arts and Sciences, 10% for Graduate School of Science, 10% for Graduate School of Frontier Sciences, etc.

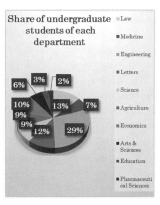

だきます。従来本学を Todai と称してきましたが、Todai は海外では非常に覚えにくいため、現在は英語での一般的な呼称として U-Tokyo を用いています。

本学は総合大学として高い評価を得ています。10学部、15研究科、11研究所を擁し、ほぼ全ての学問分野を網羅しています。学部学生は約1万4,000名、大学院学生は約1万3,000名です。学部学生と大学院学生がほぼ同数と言うこの数字が、リサーチインセンティブな大学である本学の特徴の一端を端的に示しています。

本学教員は1,300名の教授（tenured professor）、900名の准教授（tenured associate professor）、100名の特任教授（non-tenured professor）、175名の特任准教授（non-tenured associate professor）で構成されます。特任教授の大半は自然科学系の学部に属しています。これ以外にも、約1,400名の特任助教（non-tenured assistant professor）が在籍しています。この点も、リサーチインテンシブな大学の特徴を表しています。全ての終身在職権のある教員の内、人文社会科学系に属する者は約19％です。

（補足：U-Tokyo ガイドブックから以下抜粋；2013年度実績）

* 学部学生の学部別構成：工学部29％、法学部13％、文学部12％、理学部9％、医学部7％等
* 大学院学生の研究科別構成：工学系研究科24％、総合文化研究科（Arts and Sciences）10％、理学系研究科10％、新領域創成科学研究科（Frontier

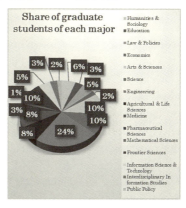

* International Students:

2,747 students [includes 2,497 graduates and 250 undergraduates].

20% of all the graduates are international students.

* Budget for FY2014:

235,840 million yen.

<Gerontology research with interdisciplinary visions and teams>

As a research university with a comprehensive coverage of various specialized fields, U-Tokyo is constantly investigating the wide-ranging problems relating to our contemporary society and human beings. One example of such investigating endeavors is a research on gerontology pursued by the Institute of Gerontology. I will explain this research succinctly. The impact brought by the population aging, which becomes prominent in Japan, is not limited to the problems in the health and welfare sectors. It creates a set of complex inter-related challenges permeating through the broad range of areas including the economy, industry and culture. For example, the more aging population increases, difficult issues of providing a proper nursing and medical care for those with dementia becomes more serious. As a result, there are rising demands for new jobs and industries to be dealt with such issues. Given these challenges, what is genuinely required is a new value system, which can take full account of not only increased personal longevity and the population aging but also a fundamental revision of conventional social mechanisms. To address a series of complex changes in a soon-coming super-aging society, it is necessary to envision and set up a newly-designed institution of research that encompasses a wide array of disciplines including medicine, nursing, science, engineering, economics, sociology, psychology, physics and education. Indeed, at the Institute of Gerontology, many projects take advantage of interdisciplinary visions and teams that can engage effectively and flexibly in research on the

Sciences) 10％等

* 留学生：留学生数は2,747名、内2,497名が大学院学生、250名が学部学生。大学院学生全体の20％は留学生。
* 2014年度収入・支出予算：予算総額は2358億4000万円

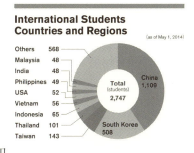

<学際的なビジョンと学際的なチーム編成によるジェロントロジー研究を展開>

　様々な専門領域を包括的に網羅する研究機関であるU-Tokyoでは、現代社会や人類に関する幅広い問題の探究に常に取り組んでいます。この探究活動の一環が、高齢社会総合研究機構が取り組んでいるジェロントロジー研究です。このジェロントロジー研究について手短にお話しいたします。日本では人口の高齢化が顕在化していますが、高齢化がもたらす影響は健康や福祉分野にとどまりません。高齢化は経済、産業、文化などの幅広い領域に浸透し、各領域が相互に関連して複雑で様々な問題を引き起こしています。例えば高齢化の進展は、認知症高齢者への適切な介護や医療提供という厄介な問題の深刻化を招いています。その結果、高齢化に係る諸問題に対処するための雇用が創出され、新たな産業が形成されつつあります。こうした課題を鑑みると、真に求められているのは新たな価値体系であり、すなわち個人の長寿化と人口高齢化のみならず、従来社会の仕組の抜本的見直しを包括的に考慮に入れた新たな価値体系が不可欠となります。目前に迫る超高齢社会における一連の複雑な変化に対するには、医学、看護学、科学、工学、経済学、社会学、心理学、物理学、教育学などの多様な学問分野を網羅する新たな研究機構の構想を練り、その機構を発足させる必要があります。実

multiple challenges in an aging society. To cope with the yet-more issues of a coming super-mature society, scientific and technological innovations have been strongly required to meet demands from relevant industries and society at large.

\<Active collaborations among a rich variety of academic disciplines\>

In response to the evolving IT society, a field of information science has been developed and now it has established a strong presence that is almost equal to that of conventional fields of science and engineering. Also, in a field of life science, a diverse range of disciplines ranging from basic medical research to regenerative medicine has been vigorously explored. As a result, there has been a increasing opportunities for collaborative research with medicine and engineering. Some collaborative research may not directly contribute to industrial or technological applications. However, it is important to conduct research based on purely scientific curiosity or visionary dreams toward the desirable future of the world we aim for. For example, there are collaborative research activities underway in the areas of physics and mathematics that explore a origin of the universe through studies of dark matter and dark energy in space. We take particular pride in being involved in such collaborative research endeavors which have been generously supported both by the government and private foundation.

Studies in humanities and social sciences play significant roles in widening and deepening our contemplation on the future of a society and the meaning of human existence from diverse viewpoints of philosophy, institutions, economics and ecosystems. In particular, even if it might be sometimes difficult to demonstrate direct and practical benefits of the humanities to society at large, the humanities are vital academic disciplines for understanding intellectual, cultural and spiritual society and also for strengthening the foundations that buttress human existence and our society.

際に高齢社会総合研究機構では、学際的なビジョンと学際的なチーム編成という利点を活かし、高齢社会が抱える諸課題の研究に効率的かつ柔軟に取り組むことで複数のプロジェクトを推進しています。来るべき超成熟社会での多くの問題に対処すべく、関連産業や社会全般からは、科学や技術分野での革新が強く求められています。

<多種多様な学問分野間でのアクティブなコラボレーション>

　IT社会の発展に呼応する形で情報科学分野は大きな進歩を遂げ、いまや従来の科学分野や工学分野とほとんど肩を並べるまでの確固たる存在感を確立するまでになりました。また生命科学分野では、基礎医学から再生医療に至るまでの多様な学問領域が盛んに研究されています。その結果、医学と工学の共同研究の機会は拡大しつつあります。これら共同研究の全てが、産業あるいは技術に直接応用されるとは限りません。しかし科学的探求心、あるいは将来を見据えた夢に基づき、我々が思い描く将来像を目指して研究を進めることは有意義なことです。例えば、宇宙に存在するダークマター（暗黒物質）やダーク（暗黒）エネルギーの研究を通じて宇宙の起源を解明する領域では、物理学と数学の共同研究活動が実施されています。本学は、政府及び民間基金双方からの寛大な支援の下にこの共同研究活動に参加していることを大いなる誇りとしています。

　人文社会科学研究は、哲学、法制度、経済学、生態系などの多様な観点を通じ、社会の将来像や人間の存在意義への考察を拡げて深める上で、重要な役割を果たします。人文学は、社会全般に役立つ直接的な便益を提示することが時に難しい学問分野ではありますが、それでも尚、知的、文化的、精神的社会を理解し、人間存在や我々の社会を支える基盤を強固なものとする上では特に不可欠な分野です。

　近年、多種多様な学問分野間でのアクティブなコラボレーションが盛んに行われようになりました。このようなコラボレーションへの参加は、

In recent years, active collaborations among a rich variety of academic disciplines have become prominent. The researchers participating in such collaborations come not only from the fields of natural science. There are also a growing number of collaborations based on a wide range of expertise in natural science, humanities and social science. Among those active collaborations are, as I have already noted, gerontology and research on sustainability which deal with contemporary issues by employing expertise in the fields of medical study, physics, bioethics and also environment and life science. Such active and interdisciplinary collaborations have great significance if we are to challenge the complex issues emerged with a a coming super-mature society. Consequently, I believe our university must further accelerate our endeavors to demonstrate its strength as the comprehensive, research-intensive, and inclusive university. Thank you very much.

Thank you for the question as to a variety of projects conducted in the University of Tokyo about the population aging issues. I'm happy to answer how these research results will be able to be brought to Japan and the rest of the world. Our research in a field of gerontology in particular is sometimes called as the "research in action" or "active research", which means a useful combination of the academic disciplines with "field research". The members of Institute of Gerontology are not confined to the research lab or office but they are very active to go out to the field; for example, they visited the area suffered from the Great East Japan Earthquake. The important thing in producing the result of research is not only to do research in the lab or office but to develop research in the field in the different places in the world. Each place presents a different issue, along with common issues with the rest of the places, and a proposed solution to the issue should be customized so as to meet the needs of each fields. My idea for educating our

自然科学分野の研究者に限ったことではありません。自然科学、人文学、社会科学などの様々な分野の専門家によるコラボレーションの数も増えつつあります。このようなアクティブなコラボレーションには、先ほど述べたジェロントロジー研究や持続可能性の研究があり、医学、物理学、生命倫理学に加え、環境科学及び生命科学分野の専門家が参加して現代社会の諸問題の解決に当たっています。来るべき超成熟社会に伴い生ずる複雑な課題に立ち向かうに際し、アクティブかつ学際的なこのようなコラボレーションは極めて重要な意味を持ちます。したがって本学は、総合大学として、またリサーチインセンティブかつ包括的研究を進める大学としての強みを明確に示すための取組を一層強化しなければならないと思っています。以上です。

　東京大学が実施する様々な高齢化問題プロジェクトに関し、ご質問いただきありがとうございます。この研究結果を、日本やその他諸外国にいかに還元し得るかについてお答えいたします。本学では、研究の中で特にジェロントロジー分野の研究を、行動を伴う研究（research in action）あるいはアクティブ研究（active research）と呼んでいます。これは、学問分野と「フィールド研究」とを有効に組み合わせるという意味です。高齢社会総合研究機構のメンバーは、研究室やオフィスに閉じこもることはせずに、東日本大震災の被災地域を訪問するなど、大変積極的にフィールドに出かけていきます。研究成果をあげる上で大切なことは、研究室やオフィスで研究するだけでなく、世界各地の様々なフィールドで研究を発展させることです。地域はそれぞれに、他の地域と共通の問題に加えてその地域固有の問題を抱えています。各地域の要望に合わせた独自の解決策を提示すべきです。学生に教室外での学習を促し、研究者に研究室外での研究を促すことが、従来型の学術研究方法と様々なフィールド研究手法とを組み合わせる重要性を改めて認識することにつながると私は考えています。これは極めて大切なことです。以上です。

students and encouraging our researches to go out to the other places is to remind the importance of combining the traditional styles of academic research and diverse methods of field research. That is the key. Thank you.

1.2 University of Oxford
Alison Beale

First of all, I would like to pass on my apologies on behalf of our Vice Chancellor, Professor Andrew Hamilton. He had to go overseas on urgent business, but he was very much looking forward to this session and he passes on his sincere apologies and very best regards to everyone.

The University of Oxford is the oldest university in the English speaking world and as such is very well known throughout the world for various reasons. It has a world-wide reputation for its strength in Humanities, its libraries, museums and collections and also for having produced many world leaders. It has produced 26 of the UK's Prime Ministers – in fact of all the elected Prime Ministers in the UK who have been university educated, the last one who was not educated at Oxford was in about 1920. We have also produced over 30 international world leaders. So we have got a very long history of producing leaders in the university.

Some other characteristics of the University of Oxford are less known, for example that in addition to its ancient history, it is also a very dynamic, research-intensive, and very modern and contemporary university. For example, it has more world-leading academics than any other UK University. In the UK we recently had the results of the latest Research Excellence Framework Exercise, and they demonstrated that we have real strength in research at the university, particularly in areas such as Medical Sciences and Mathematics. In Medicine, we have been ranked number one in

1.2 Oxford 大学
アリソン ビール

　最初に、本学の学長アンドリュー ハミルトン教授に代わってお詫びを申し上げます。急な用事ができたため、大変楽しみにしていた本フォーラムを欠席せざるを得ませんでした。私が代わってご説明いたしますので、よろしくお願いします。

　本学は英語圏で最古の大学であり、その名はさまざまな面で遍く世界に知れ渡っています。その優れた人文科学、図書館、更に、博物館と収蔵品の数々はよく知られており、また、リーダー育成を目指す大学としても名を馳せています。選挙で選出され、大学で修学した英国首相の内、オックスフォード大学出身者でない者が選出されたのは1920年頃が最後だと思います。このように本学にはリーダー輩出の大変長い歴史があります。

　オックスフォード大学が非常に活発なリサーチインテンシブな大学であり、現代的かつ最新鋭の大学でもあること、また、英国の大学の中で世界トップクラスの教員を最も多く擁していることはあまり知られていません。先ごろ英国で大学の研究を評価する REF（Research

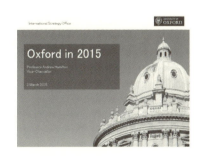

world rankings consistently for about 3 years now. Sciences are a great strength of the University. Another characteristic that is less well-known in that we are also a very international university. Now more than 50% of our students come from outside the UK, particularly at graduate level, and we have a very international student body and also a very international faculty.

<Students and faculty members>

In terms of our student numbers, as you can see from this graph, we have approximately 22,000 students, roughly half of whom are undergraduates and half of whom are postgraduates. In terms of what they study around 14% are studying Medical Sciences which makes it a very big school. The rest of our students are split relatively evenly between the Social Sciences, Humanities and a Division called Mathematical, Physical and Life Sciences.

We have a large academic and administrative staff. In total, we have almost 12,000 staff in the University. As you can see from this graph about 15% are Academic staff, and 35% roughly are Research staff, and then we have a number of other teaching and research support and other administrative functions.

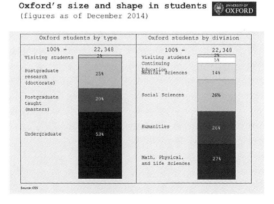

Excellence Framework）が実施され、本学の研究が再び高く評価されると同時に、特に医学と数学で高い評価を得ました。医学に関しては、今年で3年連続だと思いますが、第1位を獲得しています。医学は本学の卓越した強みであり、本学にとって非常に重要な学科となっています。また、本学は大変国際的な大学でもあります。特に大学院レベルでは学生の50％超が英国以外から来ており、学生構成は極めて国際的で、教員も国際色豊かです。

＜学生と教職員＞

学生数ですが、このグラフが示すとおり約2万2,000名が在籍し、およそ半数が学部学生、残り半数が大学院学生です。学生の専攻に関してですが、本学の全科目のうち14％の学生が医学コースで学んでいます。これは医学が非常に大きな学科であるためです。残りの学生は社会科学、人文科学、そして我々が数学、自然科学、生命科学と呼ぶ分野にほぼ等分されています。

また、本学には大変多くの教職員がいます。その総数は1万1,000名超、およそ1万2,000名です。このグラフからお分かりのとおり、約15％が教員、約35％が研究員です。その他、教育と研究のサポート要員、及び管理部門職員を多数有しています。

本学では2018年までの戦略構想を策定、研究と教育の両面で世界を先導することを目指し、国内及びグローバルなレベルの双方で社会に貢献する方法により取り組みたいと考えています。すなわち本学は英国の機関としてだけではなく、グローバルな規模で世界に貢献し、世界が今後直面するグローバルな課題や社会と向き合う機関として自らを捉えています。

＜増大する外部研究資金＞

最後に、研究資金の調達に関して述べたいと思います。本学では外部

We have a strategic plan for the university that stretches until 2018 and our major aim is to lead the world in both research and education, and we want to do this in ways that benefit society both on a national level but

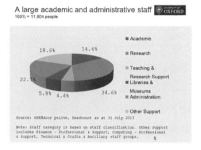

also at the global level. So we see ourselves very much as not just a UK institution, but as an institution that serves the world on a global scale, and that looks at global issues that society and the whole world are going to face.

<Increasing external research budget>
Finally, I would like to just mention about research funding. We receive a large amount of external income for research and this graph this gives a breakdown of the research funding that we receive. As you can see the amount of external funding we receive has been growing. From 2009-2010 until 2013-2014, there was a big increase. One thing that is significant is that the percentage of research funding that comes from the UK, has gone down from 77% to 71%. We are getting a larger amount of research income overall, and also a larger proportion of that is coming from outside the UK, which is a very significant factor in our University.

Thank you for the question. I'd like to say something about the role of the Colleges in the structure of the University.

In the University of Oxford, as well as in Cambridge, we have a relatively unique system – the College system - and it is works as a kind of matrix system. All faculty members and all students belong to their academic department where they are surrounded by specialists from their field, and research very deeply into their

から多額の研究資金の提供を受けています。このグラフは我々が受取る研究資金の提供内訳を示しています。ご覧のとおり調達総額は増加しています。2009-2010年から2013-2014年の間に調達総額が大幅に増えてい

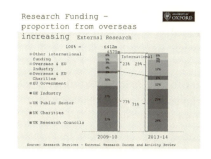

ます。これに加えて本学にとって非常に重要と思われるのは、英国内からの研究資金提供の割合が左側のグラフでは77%でしたが（右のグラフでは）71%に下がっていることです。本学が受取る研究資金総額が増加していると同時に、英国外からの資金提供割合も上昇しているのです。これは本学にとって極めて有意義なことです。

ご質問いただきありがとうございます。「カレッジの役割」についてお答えします。

オックスフォード大学及びケンブリッジ大学では、カレッジシステムという、他校に比べ独特の体制をとっています。これはマトリックス構造のような体制です。全ての教員（Faculty）と全ての学生は学科（Department）に属します。学生は各学科の専門家に囲まれながら自身の教科を深く研究します。同時に全ての学生はカレッジにも属し、そこでは活発な指導が行われます。概してカレッジはより学際的な教育研究の中心拠点となっています。つまり、全ての教員と学生は学科とカレッジの両方に属し、学科では深みを追求し、カレッジでは幅を提供します。ここに記載した数字は全職員を表しており、その全てが大学とカレッジの両方に属しています。

学部レベルの教育指導は、大変ユニークで、マンツーマンのチュートリアル（個別指導）システムの下、各カレッジで行われます。しかし、各

subject. They also however all belong to a College at the same time. This is where much of the undergraduate teaching takes place, and Colleges are generally more interdisciplinary centres of academia. So all faculty and all students belong both to departments and to colleges, so the department provides the depth and the college provides the breadth.

In terms of actual teaching, at undergraduate level this takes place in the Colleges. We have a very unique and intensive system of Tutorials, where our academics provide one-on-one teaching to students. All examinations however are set at the University level. This very intensive and structured tutoring is one of the key reasons we are able to develop world leaders.

The next question is, what is the difference between Academic and Research staff? Academic staff undertake both teaching and research in the University and therefore most of our professors would fall into this category. As the graph shows 14.6% of staff fall into this category. On the other hand Research staff take part in research only and do not undertake any teaching. Postdocs for example would fall into this category.

One other thing to bear in mind is that the terminology we use for academic staff varies from Japan and some other countries. The title of "Professor" for example is used quite sparingly in Oxford and the UK in general, and we have posts such as lecturers and readers that in other countries may be termed "Associate Professors" or even "Professors"

1.3 Ecole Centrale Nantes
Arnaud Poitou

Ecole Centrale Nantes is a much smaller institution focused on engineering. Nantes is located in the west of France and is its fifth largest city. Nantes has about 45,000 students and among these

カレッジ (College) の学生のすべての試験は大学 (University) でまとめて行われます。これは昔から行われてきたとても複雑な仕組で、進化を遂げながら続けられてきました。しかし、本学では教員と学生とが一対一で向き合うこの極めて密度の濃い個別指導こそがリーダー育成を実現する上で最も重要なものであると考えています。

続いて、指導に係る教員 (Academic) と研究員 (Research) の違いについてです。研究員は指導をしていません。図中で14.6%というのは個別指導を担当するカレッジのフェロー (Fellow) を指すと私は理解しています。その肩書きは、講師ですが、少し異なります。 オックスフォード大学での教員 (tenured) と有期雇用 (non-tenured) 教員の捉え方は少々異なっていますが、一般的に申し上げて、この14.6%は教員であり、学部学生への個別指導の責任を負うカレッジのフェローを指しています。

一方、研究員は、おそらくカレッジ内での指導の責任を負わず、学科に机のある者の方が多いと思われます。

英国では、教授の肩書を持つ者は極めて少なく、したがって14.6%はフェローという肩書だと思います。研究員はおそらく他の肩書であると思いますが、それはフェローでも教授でもありません。英国で用いる用語は海外とは大きく異なると思います。我が国では教授という肩書は、極めて限定して用いられます。

1.3 エコール サントラル ナント校
アルノー ポワトー

エコール サントラル ナントは工学に特化した非常に小規模な教育機関です。ナントはフランス西部に位置する5番目に大きな都市です。ナン

students only around 2000 study at Centrale Nantes.

Just a few words to explain the French system, which is quite distinctive, perhaps even more so than the Oxford colleges. It is based on what we call "Grande Ecoles", a system, which is sometimes difficult to explain abroad. Maybe we will change the system one day, but it still works. So, a few words of explanation:

This table shows the French educational system. On the left hand side, you have the European system, which is 3 years of bachelor study "L", 2 years of masters "M" and 3 years of PhD "D". This system is recommended by the European Bologna Process. At Centrale Nantes, we have a 5-year integrated bachelor/master degree. It is a general engineering program taught in French. Within this integrated bachelor/master degree, the first two years are accomplished prior to Centrale Nantes in, what are called, "classes Preparatoires", where students prepare for the national competitive entrance examinations for French engineering schools, which include Central Nantes. Thus, at Centrale Nantes, we only have students at third year bachelor, master and PhD levels. Some of them study general engineering, but we also offer some specialist engineering courses like international masters taught in English as well as PhDs.

<Students and faculty members>

Now, some figures about our institution, founded in 1919. We have just over 2000 students and considerably fewer academics than the other institutions around the table: 150 tenured academic staff, 100 untenured academic staff, 300 PhD students, but also 250 external lecturers from industry and 150 administrative and technical staff. An important point for us is that 30% of our students come from abroad. They are from 60 different nationalities

ト市にはおよそ4万5,000名の学生がいますが、このうちエコール サントラル ナントの学生はわずか2,000名程度です。

ここでフランスの教育制度を簡単にご説明します。フランスの教育制度は、おそらくオックスフォード大学のカレッジにもまして独特な制度です。グランゼコールと称する、海外の方にはなかなか説明しづらい制度に基づいています。この制度は今後変わると思いますが、現時点ではまだ機能しているので、簡単にご説明します。

右図は、フランスの教育制度を示しています。左端が欧州の制度で、Lで示す3年間の学士課程、Mで示す2年間の修士課程、Dで示す3年間の博士課程から成ります。この制度は欧州のボローニャ・プロセスが推

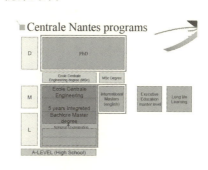

奨しています。エコール サントラル ナントでは、5年間の学士修士統合学位(integrated bachelor/master degree)を設けています。これは総合工学のプログラムで、講義はフランス語で行われます。この学士修士統合学位課程の最初の2年間はエコール サントラル ナント入学前に履修します。これは「準備級(classes preparatory)」と称され、学生はこの2年間でエコール サントラル ナントを含むフランスの工科大学に入学するための難しい国家入学試験の準備を進めます。エコール サントラル ナントに在籍するのは、学士課程の3年生、修士課程および博士課程の学生のみです。本校では、総合工学に加え、英語で講義を行う国際修士課程や博士課程などの専門工学課程も設けています。

<学生と教職員>

ここで、エコール サントラル ナントに関する数字をいくつかご紹介し

and their numbers are increasing. We have 10 international master degrees taught in English and we are very much involved with other European institutions through programs such as Erasmus Mundus. The last figure, which is

■ Centrale Nantes Key Figures
- Founded 1919 – Public Engineering school (Ministry of HE&R)
- Engineering, Masters & PhD
- 2050 graduate students
- 11000 alumni
- 550 Professors and researchers
- 250 external lecturers from industry
- 150 administrative and technical staff
- 30% of international students (+50% since 2008)
- 10 international master degrees (in english)
- 3 Erasmus Mundus Master degrees, 1 Erasmus Mundus Doctorate
- 10 EMA2 Partnership as partners, 3 as Coordinator
- 2 EMA3
- 100% of students study abroad (double degree, internship or exchange)

important for us, is that 100% of our students spend at least one semester –often up to a year- abroad. We intend for some of our future students to spend longer periods abroad, for example, 2 years in countries like Japan at Keio University, or in Tokyo.

\<Activity as part of the Ecoles Centrale group\>

Centrale Nantes is part of the Ecoles Centrale group, which brings together five campuses in France. They are located in Paris, Lyon, Lille, Marseille and Nantes. These five French campuses are supplemented by four branch campuses abroad. So, the first is in China where we have Ecole Centrale Beijing. The second is in Hyderabad in India; the third is due to open in September in Casablanca, Morocco; and very probably the fourth will open either next year or the year after in Mauritius to address growth in Africa and the Indian Ocean. All of these Ecoles Centrale are organized in the same way; they share the same goals and the same very selective entry requirements. They all subscribe to the same idea that it makes sense for some engineers to receive a general engineering education.

ます。設立は1919年で、2,000名強の学生が学んでいます。教員数は本日お集まりの皆様の大学と比べ大幅に少なく、終身在職権のある教員は150名、有期雇用の教員は100名です。博士課程の学生数は300名です。また250名の外部講師を産業界から招聘しており、管理および技術部門の職員は150名です。本校にとって重要なのは、学生の30%が留学生である点です。60ものさまざまな国々の学生が在籍し、その数は増加しています。英語で講義を行う10の国際修士課程を設け、「エラスムス・ムンドゥス(Erasmus Mundus)」などのプログラムを介して欧州各教育機関と深く関わっています。最後に、本校にとって重要な数字となるのは、学生の100%が少なくとも1学期間は海外で学ぶことです。この期間が1年に及ぶこともしばしばで、本校は将来的にこの期間を拡大し、例えば2年間にわたり、日本の慶應義塾大学や東京大学などで学生を学ばせたいと考えています。

<エコール サントラル グループとしての活動>

　エコール サントラル ナントは、フランスに5つのキャンパスを擁するエコール サントラル グループの1つです。キャンパスは、パリ、リヨン、リール、マルセイユ、ナントにあります。本グループは、フランスにあるこれら5校に、海外の4つの分校を加えて構成されます。1校目は中国にあるエコール サントラル 北京(北航中法工程師学院)です。2校目はインドのハイデラバードにあり、3校目をモロッコのカサブランカにこの9月に開校します。そして、アフリカやインド洋沿岸地域の成長に対応すべく、おそらく来年あるいは再来年に4校目をモーリシャスに開校する予定です。これら全てのエコール サントラル校は、同様の運営体制を敷いています。すなわち、同一の目標を掲げ、極めて厳格な同一の入学要件を課し、総合工学を学ぶことがエンジニアにとって有意義であるとする理念を共有しています。

　次に、エコール サントラル グループの全学生の進路の主な業種につ

Main Sectors for Recruitment

Let's look at the main recruitment sectors for our Ecoles Centrale Group students. As you can see, these statistics show that our students find employment in the main active sectors of French or international engineering activity. We also note that some of our new graduates - 10% on average - find a job in a non-engineering sector like finance, business or insurance. Furthermore, all of our statistics show that there is no strict correlation between a student's specialization and the sector of recruitment.

To better understand the pedagogical choice that we have made, it is interesting to mention the main positions held by our alumni. Around 60% of our alumni are responsible for managing industrial projects, around 20% occupy positions in research and development, and about 10% - which is rather high – hold positions of company CEO or board member. Finally around 10% - a figure we would like to see increase – are entrepreneurs.

<Educate future leaders>
Next, I would like to focus on the link between management and engineering –a key point for us – by looking at the academic background of those responsible for running the 40 largest French companies (Known as the CAC40 in France). It was observed that 28

いて見ていきます。グラフからお分かりのとおり、本校の学生は、フランスや世界各国で主流の工学系主要業種に従事しています。また、エコール サントラル グループ新卒者のうち平均10%が金融、ビジネス、保険などの工学系以外の業種に進んでいることが分かります。更に本校の全ての統計から、学生の専門分野と進路先の業種とは厳密には関連しないことが分かっています。

本校が取り組んでいる教育方針や方法をより深くご理解いただくために、本校の卒業生が就いている主な地位をご紹介するのも面白いと思います。本校卒業生の約60%は産業界の諸活動を管理監督する任に就いています。約20%は研究開発に携わり、10%程度は会社のCEOや取締役などの高い地位に就いています。そして残りの約10%は起業家となっており、本校はこの数字を拡大していきたいと思っています。

＜将来のリーダーを育成する教育＞

次に、CAC40銘柄に指定されているフランスの大企業40社の経営陣の学歴を用いて、キーポイントであるマネジメントと工学の関係に言及したいと思います。この40社のうち28社のCEOもしくはマネージングディレクターは工学を修了しており、この28名のうち25名が総合工学の履修者です。うちエコール サントラル グループの出身者は7名、エコール サントラル以外の工学教育機関であるパリ国立高等鉱業学校出身者が2名、そして、おそらくフランスで最難関の工学教育機関であるエコール ポリテクニーク出身者は16名です。この25名を除く残り3名は、専門工学教育を受けたエンジニアです。工学系以外の学歴を有する残り12名のうち8名はビジネススクール出身者で、うち7名は超難関のフランスHEC経営大学院の出身、1名はエセック経済商科大学院大学（ESSEC）の卒業生です。海外のビジネススクールの卒業生は3名です。残り1名は高等教育の学位を修得していませんが、非常に精力的に活動しているCEOです。

out of those 40 CEOs or managing directors were engineering graduates. 25 of the 28 had followed a general engineering program; including seven from Ecoles Centrale Group, two from Ecole des Mines de Paris, another engineering school, and sixteen from Ecole Polytechnique, which is probably the most selective engineering school in France. The other three are specialist engineers. Of the remaining twelve without an engineering background, eight are business studies graduates; seven HEC, a highly selective business school, and one from Essec business school; three graduated abroad and one has no higher education diploma despite being a very active CEO.

As the diagram shows, we offer an engineering program that is quite distinctive because we aim to educate future industrial leaders. In this regard, you have here, roughly speaking, the weightings of the different subjects in the curriculum. You can see that half of the curriculum in our engineering schools relates to scientific subjects – split evenly between fundamental sciences and engineering sciences. The other half relates to professional training, management, and social sciences. Another way of looking at the picture is to break it down by learning environment. Over one third of the program is devoted to courses, more than a quarter to internships in industry or abroad and roughly a quarter to project works, team activities, workshops and conferences. Finally, I would like to point out that we pay special attention to associative activities and sports because we believe that these form part of the training.

Centrale Nantes is proud of its research capacity. We have 300 PhD students which is the average number in the Ecoles Centrale group. 80% of PhDs are completed in collaboration with companies, 50% within companies. 10% are international joint PhDs and within these PhD programs we provide 300 hours of academic and professional courses.

第1部　国際学長フォーラム

これらの数字からお分かりいただけるとおり、本校は他とは明らかに一線を画す教育を展開しています。本校が将来の産業界のリーダー育成を目的としているからです。この点に関し、本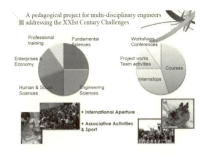
校のカリキュラムの科目構成の概要をお話します。ご覧のとおり、工学教育機関である本校のカリキュラムの半分は科学に関する科目で、これを基礎科学と工学科学とで等分に分け合っています。科学以外の残り半分は、職業訓練、マネジメントおよび社会科学に関する科目です。本校の実情をご覧いただくために、学習環境による分類という別の切り口からご説明します。本校はプログラムの3分の1以上を講義に割き、4分の1以上を企業あるいは海外で行うインターンシップに充てています。また、約4分の1をプロジェクトワーク、チーム活動、ワークショップ及び会議に充当しています。最後に、本校は関連活動やスポーツを訓練の一環と捉え、大いに注力していることを付け加えさせていただきます。

エコール サントラル ナントは優れた研究体制を有しています。博士課程に在籍する学生は300名で、これはエコール サントラル グループでは平均的な数字です。博士論文の80%は企業との共同研究によるもので、50%が企業内での研究、10%が海外機関との共同研究です。博士課程プログラムでは、300時間の一般教育と職業教育の課程を設けています。

学生のモビリティに関し、2つご質問を受けました。第1は、留学生を対象とした英語での授業に関して、第2は本校の学生の100%を海外で学ばせる理由についてです。

最初の質問についてですが、本校では留学生に2つの選択肢、すな

I have two questions regarding student mobility. The first concerns the provision of classes taught in English for international students. The second refers to the reason why 100% of our students study abroad.

In response to the first question, we offer both possibilities; that is some international students attend courses in French and some in English. Most of the courses are toughed in French for those students undertaking a double degree with us – these students spend two years in Nantes, and they learn French first. In contrast, the master's degree courses are taught in English to international and French students alike. This is easier, for example, for students arriving from India or Japan, than following lectures in French.

Concerning the second question and why, 100% of our students to study abroad. This is because, first of all, we live in a globalized world, but this is not the only reason. It is because – and we will speak about that in the second round-table - we believe that our students have to be more adaptable now than before, and we believe that the best way to enhance their adaptability is to give them the opportunity to be completely immersed in a different system, a different culture, a different language. We have come to realize that this international experience is not only interesting because of the particular country they live in, but mostly because they gain experience in adapting to very different systems.

Finally, I should mention that international placements, be they through internships or double degree programs, are compulsory. A student cannot graduate without having spent at least one semester – in fact, a year – abroad. We have a special coordinator for international study. Some of you know him, Professor Bennis.

わちフランス語または英語による受講の両方の選択肢を提供しています。本校でダブルディグリー (Double Degree) を修得する留学生の大半が、フランス語で講義を受講します。この留学生はナントで2年間過ごし、最初にフランス語を学習します。これに対し修士課程では、留学生に対してもフランス人の学生に対しても同様に英語で講義を行います。例えばインドや日本などから、フランス語教育を受けずに直接留学する学生にとっては、フランス語の講義についていかなくてよい修士課程は、より容易な選択肢となります。

2つ目のご質問は、本校が100％の学生を海外で学習させる理由についてです。第1に我々がグローバル社会に生きていることが挙げられますが、理由はこれだけではありません。第2の理由は、学生にはいま、従来に増して適応力が求められていると本校が考えているからです。全く異なる仕組、文化、言語の中にどっぷりと浸る機会を学生に与えることが、学生の適応力を伸ばす最良の方法となると信じているからです。これについては、第2セッションの全体討論で討議されると思います。本校は、こうした海外での経験が有意義であるとの見解に達しています。特定の国での生活経験が学生にとって有益だからというだけでなく、それにも増してこの海外経験は、全く異なる仕組に適応する経験を学生に積ませる機会となるからです。

最後に、インターンシップであれ共同学位プログラムであれ、本校では海外学習を必修としている点について説明します。本校の学生は最低でも1学期間、実際には約1年間の海外経験なくしては卒業することはできません。

本校では海外学習に関する専任のコーディネーターを配しています。ご存じの方がおられると思いますが、ベニス教授 (Prof. F. Bennis) がそうです。

1.4 National University of Singapore
Chorh Chuan Tan

Singapore like many Asian economies, has progressed rapidly over the last 50 years. If you look at our GDP from say 1960 to 2014, it has grown about 400 times in nominal terms. At the same time, our population is ag-

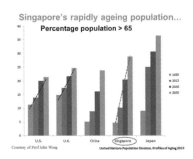

ing very rapidly. This is illustrated in the figure which shows the percentage of the population above 65 years of age in 1980, 2013, 2030 (projected) and in 2050 (projected). You can see that Singapore has one of the steepest slopes in terms of aging, hence we are keen to learn from societies like Japan which has been noted, are already facing the issues that will come to us very soon.

Coming to the National University of Singapore, the roles that we have played as the national university have evolved in tandem with the country's rapid development. In the 1960s, Singapore's economy involved low-wage very labor intensive activities such as making toys and garments, but in successive decades, we engaged in higher skilled and more complex manufacturing and services. In the late 90s, the government decided that we needed to move more quickly to become a knowledge-intensive economy and society, developing our own knowledge, innovations and businesses. In line with these shifts, NUS evolved from a predominantly teaching institution training manpower for the economy, to a comprehensive research intensive university which provided knowledge and innovations to drive economic and societal advancement.

We are a publically funded university, although we are

1.4　シンガポール国立大学

チョウ　チョア　タン

　多くのアジア諸国同様、シンガポールはこの50年で急速な経済発展を遂げました。例えば1960年から2014年までの我が国の名目GDPは、およそ400倍に拡大しました。同時に、高齢化も極めて急速に進行しています。これは、1980年、2013年、2030年（予測値）、2050年（予測値）の65歳以上人口の割合を記す左図が示すとおりです。ご覧のとおり、シンガポールは最も急激な高齢化カーブを描いている国の1つです。それゆえ我々は、日本のような社会から積極的に学びたいと思っています。先ほどのお話にもありましたが、日本が既に直面している課題がシンガポールのものとなる日が目前に迫っているからです。

　シンガポール国立大学（NUS）に話を転じます。国立大学である本学の役割は、シンガポール国家の急速な発展にあわせて進化を遂げてきました。1960年代のシンガポール経済は、玩具や衣料品製造をはじめとする、低賃金かつ極めて労働集約型の活動によるものでした。その後数十年間は、高度な技術を伴うより複雑な製造業やサービス業を展開してまいりました。シンガポール政府は90年代後半に、自国の知識の育成、技術革新の促進、事業の振興を進め、知識集約型の経済および社会への移行を加速させるとの決断を下しました。NUSは従来、経済活動を支える労働力の訓練に軸足を置く教育機関でしたが、政府のこの転換にあわせ、包括的かつリサーチインテンシブな大学、すなわち、知識を提供して革新を起こし、経済や社会の発展を後押しする機関へと変革を遂げました。

　本学の設立形態は法人ですが、公的資金の提供を受けています。資金提供の60数パーセントは依然として政府が占めています。本学は比

structured as a company. We receive about 60 odd percent of our funding from the government still. We have a relatively large enrolment with about 28,000 undergraduates and about 10,000 graduate students. We have about 1600 tenure-track

faculty about 1600 as well as additional educator track and practice track faculty. We also have lecturers, senior lecturers and other teaching staff, so the total number of academic staff is around 3000. These do not include research faculty and staff lab and clinical faculty. Of the tenure-track faculty, about a third are in the humanities and social sciences.

I interpreted the "current status" as referring to the things we are doing now, and the "future status" as referring to the things we are working on for the future. With your permission, I would take a couple of minutes to talk briefly of some of the things that we have been working on for several years which are directed at the issues of the super-mature society and globalization more generally. I think President Hamada has made a very important case for multi-disciplinary research necessary to tackle problems like super-mature societies but there is the challenge of how to make it work. You can form an institute but the problem is many of these institutes may become too broad or get fixed on some research programs, which are difficult to adapt over time. It is also hard to bring other types of disciplines like city planning, architecture, behavior sciences into these programs.

We experimented with various approaches, of which the most promising has been the integrated research cluster. We launched this initiative about 5 years ago, so it is too early to tell if it is really

較的大規模な学生数を擁し、約 2 万 8,000 名の学部学生と約 1 万人の大学院学生が在籍しています。教員は終身在職権を持つ者と有期雇用の者を合わせて約 1,600 名、その他にもエデュケータートラック(educator track)、プラクティストラック (practice track) の教員がいます。講師、上級講師、その他教職員もおり、教職員を合計するとおよそ 3,000 名程度となります。この 3,000 名には、研究員、職員や医療関連の教員は含まれません。終身在職権を持つ教員及び有期雇用教員のおよそ 3 分の 1 が人文・社会科学の教員です。

私はこれまでに「現状」、すなわち本学が現在取り組んでいることと、「将来像」、すなわち将来に向けて取り組んでいることをお話ししてまいりました。お許しいただければ少々お時間をいただき、超成熟社会やグローバル化の問題について、ここ数年来本学で幅広く取り組んでいる活動について、簡潔に説明させていただきたいと思います。超成熟社会のような問題の解決には複数の専門領域にまたがる研究が必要とされますが、これに関しては先ほど濱田総長から貴重な事例をご紹介いただきました。しかし、これをどのように実行するかが課題となります。機関を創設する方法もありますが、問題はこのような機関は研究領域を広げ過ぎる、あるいは特定の研究プログラムに固執する可能性があり、時間の経過とともに実情に沿わない機関となってしまうことです。また、都市計画、建築、行動科学などのタイプの異なる専門領域を、研究プログラムに組み込むことが難しくなります。

本学はさまざまな方法を試みましたが、その中で最も成果が高かったのは統合研究クラスター (integrated research cluster) です。この取組を開始したのはおよそ 5 年前であり、この取組の成否を判断するには時期尚早です。しかし統合研究クラスターは、教職員同士が協働し、特定領域の研究を深く掘り下げると同時に、協力してより広範な研究課題の解決に当たる上で極めて大きな成果をあげています。では、このクラスターがどのように機能しているかをご説明させていただきます。

successful but the integrated research clusters do provide very good fora for us to bring faculty together, to do deep research in specific areas and still cooperate in addressing a much larger research question. Let me explain how it works.

For example, for ageing, we set up the Virtual Institute for the Study of Aging, VISA, not the credit card, but a cluster that engages about 250 researchers in NUS working on various aspects of aging, categorized as the aging cell, the aging person and the aging society. What the Cluster does is to bring different types of researchers together, to map out what the whole group are doing and to share ideas regularly. We have small cooperative research grants, and we also try to find two ways in which we can get them to work together on big problems. One way is through the definition of a grand challenge research issue. An example could be to solve the problem of mobility of the elderly in housing estates. Another way is through testbeds, both on the campus and outside our campus.

<How to have the zoom-out, zoom-in capability>

If I can turn now to education, a key goal in NUS is to equip our students with a set of general skills that could be broadly applied across different work sectors and industries.

Intellectual breadth with rigour is also critical. I believe that many graduates of the future would benefit from developing what I would term a strong "zoom-out, zoom-in" capability. That is, to have a broad enough intellectual base so that they can join the dots and see connections between different issues, across disciplines. You need to be able to zoom out but on the other hand, you must also be able to zoom in on a specific issue or problem that is an area of focus, you must be able to go deeply into it with rigour, and where necessary, using appropriate scientific methods to frame and solve problems. The best way to develop such a capability is to combine rigorous academic programs with experiential

例えば高齢化に関して、本学は高齢化研究のためのバーチャル機構（Virtual Institute for the Study of Aging、VISA）を創設しました。クレジットカードではありませんよ。NUS で高齢化に関するさまざまな分野の研究を行う 250 名の研究員を擁するクラスターであり、この研究員が細胞の高齢化、人の高齢化、社会の高齢化に分かれて研究を行っています。本クラスターは、異なるタイプの研究員を集約し、グループ全体の活動を精緻に調整し、定期的に考えを共有する機能を担っています。少額ですが共同研究補助金を設けると共に、研究員たちが協働して大きな課題に取り組めるよう、2 つの方策を講じています。1 つ目は、大きな課題を研究対象に設定することであり、例えば住宅団地に住む高齢者のモビリティ問題の解決などが挙げられます。2 つ目は、キャンパス内外に数多くのテストベッド（試験環境）を用意することです。

＜ズームインとズームアウト能力の育成＞

次に教育に関する話をさせていただきます。NUS の重要な目標は、様々なセクターや産業に幅広く適用可能な広範なスキルを学生に習得させることです。

知識の幅広さと厳密さも不可欠です。私が「ズームアウト、ズームイン」と称する確固たる能力を習得することで、多くの学生は将来、その恩恵に浴することでしょう。すなわち、専門領域をまたいで様々な課題を関連付け、関係性を見出すには、極めて広範な知識基盤の構築が必要です。ズームアウトする能力は必要ですが、その一方で、注力すべき特定の課題や問題にズームインする能力も不可欠です。課題や問題を厳密かつ深く掘り下げ、必要とあれば科学的方法を的確に用いて問題の把握と解決に当たることが求められます。学生にズームインとズームアウト能力を習得させる最善の方法は、厳密な教育カリキュラムと経験を通じた学習とを組み合わせることです。これにより学生は、自身を取り巻く現実世界の問題や状況に、理論を適用させる力を試されることとなります。

learning, which challenges students to apply theory around real world issues and conditions.

Experiential learning is also very important to provide the opportunities that take students outside of their comfort zones and be stretched intellectually and personally. Through this process, students will also discover and develop crucial personal qualities like initiative, imagination, resilience and perseverance.

Finally, as pointed out by Professor Poitou it is very important that while constituents are global and yet they must be locally engaged. In other words, we must also have a certain sense of feeling for the local community and being genuinely engaged with it. Hence, even while NUS is very global, at the same time, we are also deeply engaged locally in Singapore.

<NUS University Town>

Experiential learning is a key element of NUS education and we have several initiatives linked to this. I will just mention one very quickly, that is NUS' University Town. Since 2011, we have built and opened in phases, an

entire new educational complex over a greenfield 19 hectare site. The physical complex is designed with interaction in mind, and the multi-use buildings combine learning spaces with sports, culture and social facilities. A major part of the University Town are the 4 Residential Colleges. Each college accommodates 600 undergraduates, and creates a distinctive living and learning community and environment. Students admitted to the Colleges are randomized to create the greatest diversity in terms of disciplines, backgrounds and for the 30% international students, range of

また経験を通じた学習は、学生を居心地のいい環境の外に引っ張り出し、知識の伸長と個人の成長を促す極めて重要な機会です。また、学生はこの経験学習を通じ、自主性、創造性、逆境からの回復力、忍耐強さなど、自身の大切な資質を見出し、その資質を伸ばすことができるのです。

　最後に申しあげたいのは、ポワトー校長のご指摘のとおり、グローバルな要素を考慮しつつも、地域に関与することが重要だという点です。別の言い方をすると、我々は、地域社会に対しても確固たる意識を持ち、地域社会にしっかりと関わる意識を持たなければならないということです。NUS は極めてグローバルな機関ですが、同時にシンガポール地域とも深い関わりを有しています。

＜ NUS 大学タウン＞

　経験を通じた学習は、NUS の教育の重要な要素であり、本学ではこの学習に関する複数の施策を実施しています。その施策の 1 つである NUS 大学タウンに関し、手短にご説明します。2011 年以降、本学は 19 ヘクタールの緑地に、全く新しい教育複合施設を建設し、段階的に拡張してきました。複合施設の建物は、交流 (interaction) することを念頭に設計され、学習空間にスポーツ、文化、社交用施設を組合せた多目的な建造物となっています。大学タウンの主要部は、4 つの居住用カレッジが占めています。各カレッジは 600 名の学部学生を収容し、特色ある居住と学習のコミュニティ及び環境を形成しています。カレッジへの入居が許可された学生は、彼らの多様性を最大にするように、学科や育ってきた環境や国籍によらず無作為に割り振られます。学生は 2 年間で、15 名から成るセミナー形式の課程を 5 つ履修します。この課程では、コミュニケーションとライティングに注力すると同時に、広範なグローバル問題も積極的に扱います。その目的は、この 15 名のグループに、世界とアジア両方の視点からグローバル問題に取り組ませることにあります。さ

nationalities. The students take 5 seminar-style courses in groups of 15, over a 2 year period. The courses focus on communications and writing, as well as on broad global issues with the goal of encouraging the group to look at these through both global as well as Asian lens. There are also a wide range of out of the classroom learning, artist in residence, many events involving external speakers such as politicians, sportsmen, artists and so on. This co-academic programs are very useful in broadening the academic interests of the students and helping them to gain self-confidence and a stronger ability to engage intellectually and personally with unfamiliar topics and situations.

1.5 Keio University
Atsushi Seike

As you may know, Keio University is the oldest private university in Japan established in 1858 by Yukichi Fukuzawa. It has now 29,000 undergraduate students in 10 Faculties from Letters to Medicine and 5000 post graduate students in 14 Graduate schools. We have about 3000 full-time faculties and about 3000 full-time staff. Our total budget, I mean, annual budget is about ¥139 billion or about $1.2 US billion. About one-third of our revenue is from tuition and another one-third from medical revenues from our hospital and the remaining one-third from various sources including research funds both from public and private sectors and donations and returns from our financial assets.

About the Japanese aging, I already told you a little bit. Japan's aging population is unprecedented in world scale. Japan's aging population has unprecedented scale in many aspects. At first, as I told you, the proportion of all the people aged 65 years

らに多種多様な教室外学習、アーティスト・イン・レジデンスプログラムや、政治家、スポーツマン、芸術家など外部の人を招いて行う各種イベントなども展開しております。学習プログラムと並行して行うこのプログラムは、学生の学問的関心を拡げ、自信を与えると共に、従来扱ったことのない題材や状況に際し、知識を駆使して自らの手で対処する力を習得させる上で、大きく貢献しています。

1.5 慶應義塾大学
清家　篤

　慶應義塾大学は日本最古の私立大学であり、福沢諭吉により1858年に創設されました。現在、学部学生は2万9,000名、文学部から医学部に至るまでの10の学部を有しています。また、大学院学生は5,000名、その研究科は14です。約3,000名の常勤教員と約3,000名の常勤職員がいます。慶應義塾の総予算、すなわち年度予算額は約2,000億円、およそ16億米ドルです。本学の収入の3分の1は授業料、3分の1は大学病院からの医療収入、残り3分の1は官民両方からの研究資金や寄付金、資産運用益などのさまざまな収入

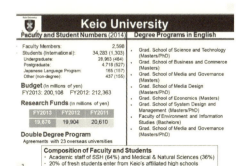

old and over is already 26%. So let me skip that part in order to save the time.

<A couple of new initiatives>

Now, let me just talk about couple of new initiatives we started. Both of them are aiming to improve the quality of research and education and expand our international activity. We have received general support from the government to do this. First is so called Program for Leading Graduate School. In terms of rapid globalization, social issues have become more complex and diversified.

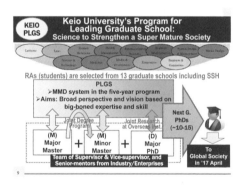

Issues related to environmental, energy resources and aging societies are deeply intertwined both on the global and on the domestic scale.

Against this backdrop, universities are expected to contribute on wide scale and deeper level through more sophisticated research and by strengthening collaborations with industry and government. In order to respond to such demands, the Ministry of

です。

　日本の高齢化に関しては先ほど既に少しお話しさせていただきました。我が国の人口の高齢化は世界に類を見ないものです。多くの面で先例のない規模で進行しています。先ほどご説明したとおり65歳以上の人口構成比率は既に26%となっています。

＜新たな2つの施策＞

　慶應義塾が取り組んでいる新たな施策を2つお話させていただきます。この2つの施策の狙いは共に研究と教育の質の向上及び大学の国際活動の拡大にあります。両施策の実施に際しては政府からの全面的な支援を受けています。第1の施策は博士課程教育リーディングプログラムと称するものです。急速なグローバル化に伴い、社会問題はより複雑化、多様化しています。環境、エネルギー資源、高齢化社会などは、グローバルな規模においても、また、国内においてもさまざまな課題が複雑に絡まり合っています。

　この状況の下で大学には、洗練された研究を通じてより広範囲にかつ深く貢献すること、また、産業界と政府との協力を強化することが期待されています。この要請に応えるため文部科学省は2011年に博士課程教育リーディングプログラムを始動させました。本プログラムは、大学を支援し、博士課程5年一貫のもとで学生を教育し、骨太の専門性をもち広い視野と独創性を備えグローバルに活躍できる高度博士人材を育成することを目指しています。このプロジェクトの一環として、慶應義塾大学からは2つのプログラムが採択されました。1つは2012年4月開講の「超成熟社会発展のサイエンス」であり、もう1つは2013年4月開講の「グローバル環境システムリーダープログラム」です。

　それぞれに特徴を持つこれら2つのプログラムでは、理系と文系を融合させた「水飲み場」環境のもと、研究科での研究および指導に加え、国際トレーニングも提供しています。また、プログラムメンバーは、教

Education, Culture, Sports, Science and Technology launched the programs for Leading Graduate School in 2011. The aim of that program is to support universities and educate doctoral level students to become active global leaders with broad perspective and creative outlook. As part of this project, two programs from Keio were selected. One is "the Science for the Development of Super-Mature Society", inaugurated in April 2012, and the other is "the Global Environmental System Leaders" in April 2013. These distinctive programs integrate the arts and sciences for both international trend as well as education and research in faculty, environment comprising members from academia, industry and government. Keio University is developing professionals equipped with high level skills necessary for all-round involvement in society beyond their own research expertise so that they can establish and implement solutions to those interwoven global challenges.

<Top Global University project has started>

In line with our continued efforts to globalize our campus, last year Keio applied for the Japanese government's grant so called Top Global University project. Keio University was fortunate enough to be selected in the top 5 category as one of Japan's top 13 universities providing world class level research and education. Under this project, Keio is committed to further social contribution as an international research university. As part of our project which is titled enhancing sustainability of global society through *jitsugaku* or science, Keio created three research and education initiatives; 'longevity', 'security' and 'creativity' which respond to critical issues that challenge the sustainability of our society mainly aging population, and increased risk to environmental, economic and regional security, and the high demand for creativity to achieve sustainable growth.

In these initiatives of longevity, and creativity, we would like to see that professors and students from all Faculties and Graduate

育研究機関、産業界、行政体の人々により構成されています。特に、グローバル企業などで豊富な経験を積んだシニアメンターが、学生に与える「気づき教育」が果たす役割は本プログラムの一つの鍵です。慶應義塾大学では、専門研究領域を超え、社会と幅広く関わる上で必要とされる高度なスキルを備えたプロフェッショナル、すなわちグローバル規模で複雑に絡み合うさまざまな課題への解決策を考え、実施できる高度博士人材を育成しています。

<スーパーグローバル大学創成への取組み>

また、継続して取り組んでいるキャンパスのグローバル化路線に沿い、昨年、スーパーグローバル大学創成支援と称される政府プロジェクトに助成金を申請しました。幸いなことに慶應義塾大学はトップ5カテゴリーに採択され、日本において世界レベルの教育研究を行う13のトップ大学の1校として認められました。このプロジェクトのもとで慶應義塾大学は国際的な研究大学として一層社会に貢献していくことを約しています。「実学(サイエンス)によって地球社会の持続可能性を高める」ことを冠したプロジェクトの一環として、3つの研究教育イニシアティブ、すなわち「長寿」、「安全」、「創造」を打ち出しました。各イニシアティブが、日本社会の持続可能性、言い換えると 高齢化、環境・経済・地域の安全への高まるリスク、持続的成長の実現に強く求められる創造性、とい

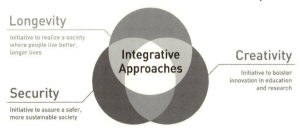

schools work together in research and education for the healthy society and more secure society and more creative society. If we can find solutions to cope with these problems, it will have many valuable policy implications for other countries which face or will face similar problems.

We have many high caliber faculties and students who are able to undertake this type of research. In each of three initiatives, we will conduct advanced research applied to solve problems through interdisciplinary approaches and use feedback from the result of other deep basic research. We will also carry out numerous evolution or education and research including expanding our joint supervision scheme with leading scholars from overseas and increasing the number of degree programs delivered in English.

In terms of the reform of human resource management, we will promote changes and employment in cross-appointment, tenure track and annual salary system. The global nature of these initiatives and reform present us with opportunities to strengthen collaboration ties with the international community through joint research and academic exchanges with world leading universities including yours. By doing so, we can improve the quality of our research and education, and as a result, we will build up a sustainable society cooperated with our international competitors. That is just a brief presentation from myself.

う重大な課題に対応しています。

　「長寿」、「安全」、「創造」という３つのイニシアティブでは、全学部、全大学院研究科の学生と教員が協力して研究教育に取り組み、より健康長寿で、より安全で安心、かつ創造力に富んだ社会を目指すことを期待しています。これら「長寿」、「安全」、「創造」への解決策を見出せれば、日本と同様の問題に直面している、あるいは、将来直面すると思われる国々の政策に貴重な示唆を与えることとなるでしょう。

　慶應義塾にはこのようなタイプの研究を実施する有能な教員と学生が大勢います。「長寿」、「安全」、「創造」の３つのイニシアティブの各々で先進的な研究を実施し、学際的アプローチによる問題解決を図ると共に、より深い基礎研究の成果のフィードバックを活用してまいります。同時に、数々の教育研究改革を実施してまいります。これには、海外の第一線で活躍されている学者との共同指導体制（Cross Appointment Professorship）の拡充や、英語で行われる学位取得課程の数を増やすことなどが含まれます。

　人材マネジメント改革に関しては、変革を推進し、クロスアポイントメント制度、テニュアトラック制度、年俸制での雇用を促進してまいります。今述べた３つのイニシアティブや改革はグローバルな性質を帯びているため、皆様の大学をはじめとする世界有数の大学との共同研究や学術交流を通じて、また、国際社会との協力を通して、慶應義塾大学が結び付きを強める機会となります。こうすることで、慶應義塾の研究教育の質を高め、その結果、海外の競合校と協力して、持続可能な社会を築いていくのです。簡単ですが、私からのプレゼンテーションは以上です。

Chapter 2
Future prospects for education and research of university
—Discuss a lot of tradeoff issues—

Fumihiko Kannari

The second session is about the future prospects because we already understand the present stage of each university. To cope with social issues in the future, we have to improve or develop the new educational work, research function platform. If you have any plan or even personal opinion, please present your idea in this session. Professor Seike, could you start?

Atsushi Seike

Let me just raise some agenda from which I would like to have a comment. Many of our colleagues, particularly President Tan raised, I think, one of the most important issues is that we are now facing many tradeoffs in fields of education and research, for example, expertise versus interdisciplinary or basic versus applied or maybe independence and collaboration. Of course, they do not necessarily complete tradeoff. Sometimes, we can make a bridge between the two and we have to do that sort of work. I am just curious to know in what way we can sort of cope with these tradeoff problems because many people including myself often say lighten up, we need to have interdisciplinary research to solve many problems and that is true, but on the other hand, interdisciplinary research is not so easy and sometimes when we do some interdisciplinary research, many of these researches would be relatively shallow ones. What we really would like to have is on one hand, we do in-depth research in each expertise and then integrate these in-depth researches into some interdisciplinary approach, but I still am not quite sure what is best way for us to build them.

第2章
大学の教育と研究の将来展望
―多くのトレードオフ問題を議論する―

神成文彦

　続けて第2セッションを始めます。各大学の現状に関してこれまでに理解が深まりましたので、第2セッションでは将来の展望について話し合います。超成熟社会における社会問題へ対処するためには、教育活動、研究機能、それらのプラットフォームの向上あるいは開発に取り組む必要があります。将来の計画、あるいは、個人的なご意見でも結構ですので、このセッションでお聞かせください。清家塾長からお願いします。

清家　篤

　まずいくつかの論点についてコメントをさせていただきたいと思います。ご出席の皆様の多く、特に、タン学長から我々が直面する非常に重要な問題が提起されました。つまり、教育研究領域で数々のトレードオフの選択を迫られているということです。例えば専門的であるべきか学際的であるべきか、基礎か応用か、あるいは単独かコラボレーションかなどです。もちろん、これらは必ずしも完全なトレードオフの関係ではありません。時には対立していると思われる2つの間を繋ぐこともできますし、また、そうしなければいけない時もあります。私はただ、こうしたトレードオフの問題にいかに対処し得るのかを知りたいのです。視野を広げて、さまざまな問題に対処するためには学際的研究が必要です、これは私自身も含め多くの人々がよく口にすることです。これは正しいことですが、一方、学際的研究はそうたやすいことではありません。学際的研究を行ったとしても、専門領域の研究と比して皮相的なものとなることが往々にしてあります。我々が本当に求める姿は、各専門領域の研究を深める一方、その後に、この深めた研究を繋げ、学際的アプローチへと

Fumihiko Kannari

Thank you professor Seike. It will be a great subject for discussion. I think one of the concepts that have been already given by Professor Tan is collaboration of the many deep research and then connect together for particular general problem. So how that is successful so far?

Chorh Chuan Tan

I would like to share three quick thoughts in the interest of time. Firstly, I think it is too early to tell if the integrative research cluster approach is really successful. However, my overall experience is that if you can find the right intellectual leaders who can galvanize enough top researchers from other fields to be engaged in the topics identified, it can be a very powerful way to bring a wide range of disciplinary expertise to tackle a large complex research question.

Secondly, I feel we have to recognize the "lifecycle" of the academic and what the key focus should be at different phases. For example, Assistant professors should be given the time and support to develop and demonstrate that they can do deep, high quality research and that they have research independence meaning that they go into fields beyond that of their Ph.D. supervisors.

Also, my sense is that we don't need all of our faculty to concentrate on delivering on multiple objectives. For example, if we could have say 15%-20% of our faculty doing exciting and truly cross-disciplinary research, this may be sufficient particularly if these are very strong research faculty. It is likely that many of these would be tenured professors or associate professors who can

統合することです。しかし、私には何が学際的アプローチ確立の最善の方法であるかが、いまだにはっきりと分かっていません。

神成文彦

　清家塾長、ありがとうございます。議論に格好のポイントです。これに対する答えの1つは、既にタン学長がご説明くださっています。それは深く掘り下げた複数の研究をコラボレーションさせ、その後これらの研究を特定の総合的な問題のために結び付ける方法です。現段階ではこの方法はどの程度うまくいっているのでしょうか？

チョウ チョア タン

　時間の関係上、私の考えを3つ、手短に述べたいと思います。

　まず1点目です。シンガポール国立大学の統合研究クラスターが実践している方法の成否を判断するには時期尚早ですが、これまでの私の経験から、次のようなことが言えます。すなわち、様々な分野のトップレベルの研究員たちを率い、発奮させ、規定した課題に取り組ませるに足る知識と知性を兼ね備えたリーダー適任者を見つけることができれば、様々な学問領域の専門家たちを集めて、広範で複雑な研究課題の解決に当たらせることが非常に有効な方法となり得る、ということです。

　次いで2点目です。私は、教員の「ライフサイクル」、およびライフサイクルの各段階で何に注力すべきかを、我々が認識する必要があると考えています。例えば、助教には、質の高い研究を深く掘り下げさせ、また研究の独立性を与えること、すなわち、彼らが博士課程で指導教授のもとで行った研究分野以外の研究を独自に行うための時間を与え、その能力を伸ばし、またその能力を立証するために支援すべきです。

　また、すべての教員が学際的研究に参入する必要はないと感じています。例えば、15～20％程度の教員が真に分野横断的で刺激的な研究を行うのであれば、この程度の割合で十分でしょう。特に、この教員が

boldly move into new areas and with them, they can bring along other people. The other faculty could remain working in disciplinary areas. In other words, it is a portfolio approach that we are after with the main criterion being that the work being produced is of high quality and impact.

Thirdly, we should try our best to create an overall environment that reduces the barriers across Faculties to collaborate. There are many ways and each of us are already doing this. Personally, I feel that the most issue is to have Deans strongly committed to high-impact work and strongly supportive of multidisciplinary research. We want deans who are there to create a collaborative environment. If you have the right environment coupled with a core of 10%-15% of faculty leaders, it creates the conditions where you can have enough people doing really interesting multidisciplinary work, alongside the larger group of the faculty who are still focused on primarily disciplinary work. As far as we are concerned that is okay. What we are interested in is that you must do good work and have a certain percentage who are doing really groundbreaking work which is consequential and influential.

Junichi Hamada

Based on my experience, I would say that there are two crucial points to be remembered in encouraging interdisciplinary research in the university.

One is derived from the observations learned through the Institute of Gerontology. This Institute sets up only a few posts for a "leader" or managing professor of research projects. In fact, the size of this Institute is not at all small, and it has more than 20

極めて優秀な研究者である場合は然りです。新たな領域へと果敢に踏み出し、同僚をこの分野へ勧誘することができる終身在職権を持った教授や准教授が、往々にしてこのような教員に該当します。これ以外の教員は、従来どおり彼らの専門領域を研究することになります。別の言い方をすると、これは一つのポートフォリオの手法であり、影響力の大きい第一級の成果が主要な基準となり、我々全体を牽引するのです。

次いで3点目です。我々は、異なる学部の教員同士がコラボレーションする際の障壁を取り除き、全体的な環境の整備に最善を尽くさなければなりません。その方法はさまざまであり、各々すでに手段が講じられています。個人的には、私は影響力の大きい成果を創出することに積極的に取り組み、専門領域を横断する研究へ支援を惜しまない学部長を得ることが、最も重要だと考えています。我々に必要なのは、共同研究環境を創りだす役割を果たす学部長です。適切な環境が整備され、ここに教員の核となる10～15％のリーダーが加われば、複数の専門領域にまたがる有益な研究に従事する人を相当数確保できると同時に、その他大部分の教員は引き続き専門領域の研究に注力する状況が実現するのです。本学に関して言うと、それで十分だと思っています。注目すべきは優れた研究を行うことであり、重大な結果をもたらし、影響力が大きく極めて画期的な研究を、一定割合の人が行うことが重要なのです。

濱田純一

私の経験ないし見解を述べさせていただきますと、大学で学際的研究を推進する際に重要なことは2点です。1点目は、高齢社会総合研究機構での経験から得た見解です。本機構の場合、若干名の研究プログラムリーダーやマネージャーを置き、20名以上の教員で構成されていますが、大半の教員の学識は従来型の学部に根差したものであり、従来型の伝統的な専門領域を出るものではありません。しかし、1名ないし

academic staff members. Most of them are rooted in and related to the existing Faculties with traditional academic disciplines. So, the point is, if we can get one "good" manager –or a few good managers-, then he or she can manage those fellow professors in a successful way and make close collaboration. At present, we invest just one or two posts for managing professors to lead research projects.

The second point I would like to bring up is that the merit of combination of interdisciplinary education and interdisciplinary research. We provide the university-wide undergraduate education programs, and the university-wide graduate programs, which include programs relating to gerontology, oceanology, and life innovation. Usually, when a new university-wide education program is set up, professors in relevant academic disciplines are recruited from various existing Faculties, and in the process of curriculum making and teaching, these professors have new opportunities to collaborate with each other. Indeed, such collaborative education activities in turn make these professors to reflect on the interdisciplinary research activities, and then lead them to the new cooperative relationship. I have already witnessed several good examples of such a cyclical phenomenon in our research and education.

Arnaud Poitou
<Develop interpersonal skills and motivation>
Concerning the question about the ability of cross disciplinarily, which is very important, we believe that for both student and staff, it is worth noting that we do not have only to educate people to know-how but also maintain the same attitude in interpersonal skills and motivation, and probably we believe and we try to go in that direction if we wish to cultivate our students in a

2名の優秀なマネージャーを得ることができれば、この教授たちをうまく管理し、うまく組み合わせることができます。本機構がそのいい事例です。現在、本機構ではプロジェクトマネージャーの任を担う教授を1、2名置き、管理監督者としての立場からその者がプロジェクト全体を管理しています。お話ししたい2点目は、学際的教育と学際的研究を組合せることです。東京大学では学部学生を対象とした全学的な学部横断教育プログラムと、同じく大学院生を対象とした全学的な大学院横断プログラムを設けており、このプログラムにはジェロントロジー、バリアフリー問題、ライフイノベーションなどがあります。このような学部横断的プログラムの実施に際しては、さまざまな学部から教授が集められています。カリキュラムの作成や指導に当たっては、さまざまな学部から参加している教授たちがコラボレーションします。その結果、このような共同活動は研究活動に影響を及ぼしています。少なくとも新たな協力関係が構築されています。本学の研究活動ではこのような現象が分かっています。

　このコラボレーションは、駒場キャンパスから始まりました。これは教養（リベラル・アーツ）学部です。リベラル・アーツは包括的な概念であり、そもそも学際的コラボレーションが期待されています。これにより駒場の教授は他の教授の活動を気にすることなく、自在に指導に当たっています 。したがって、私の印象ですが、駒場は極めて独立して存在するキャンパスだと思っています。

アルノー ポワトー
＜対人スキルとモチベーションの育成＞

　専門領域を横断する能力について述べます。これは非常に重要です。エコール サントラル ナント校では、ノウハウ教育のみならず、対人スキルやモチベーション教育も行っていることに、学生と教職員の双方が注意を払ってほしいと思います。我々はこの必要性を信じており、この方向に向かって進もうとしています。学生のこれからの人生に向け、複数の専

multidisciplinary direction in their life, it is necessary to develop interpersonal skills and motivation.

With these three key words which is 'know-how', 'interpersonal skill' and 'motivation', we can say that concerning know-how, we try to develop basic science because the science does not depend on up-to-date technologies. We develop technology because our students must be able to get from research to innovation, and we develop management skill because, as I mentioned previously, our students will have very rapidly to manage project and/or people and organization.

In terms of interpersonal skills, we believe that we have to develop hardworking. This is done through our selective system. Leadership which is cultivated in different ways, sport for example, talk activities for example, High responsibility for example, things around corporate social responsibility courses, and things like art. Concerning motivation, it is mainly done at two different levels which are personal development and are to learn about yourself. This is coaching, mentors and this is very important factor, and professional project that is to choose or create a project which is both realistic and suited for you.

That is to say, we completely agree with President Seike that multidisciplinary is sometimes dangerous because it leads to swallow knowledge. But most important thing is maybe in 10% students to be motivated.

Final talk about three main key words that are very specific of our actual period. We spoke about multidisciplinary as one. The second very important keyword for us is collaboration. Collaborative project is something new. We were used to work alone in one organization. Because probably we are faced with that especially in Europe, we spoke about European project how this works, so European project is a bit like your JSPS system but at European level. We have to create some collaborative projects between different institutions, different cultures, and we believe that it is

門分野にまたがり行動する力を身に付けさせたいのであれば、対人スキルとモチベーションの養成は欠かせません。

　ノウハウ、対人スキル、モチベーションというこれら3つのキーワードについてお話しします。ノウハウに関しては、本校では基礎科学力の養成に努めています。基礎科学は最先端技術に依らないからです。また、技術力の養成にも努めています。研究から新たな考えややり方を導きだせる力を学生に付けさせるためです。マネジメントスキルも養成しています。先ほど申しましたが、本校の学生は直ぐにでも、プロジェクト、人、組織、あるいはこれら全てを管理するよう求められるからです。

　対人スキルに関して、本校では勤勉な姿勢の養成が必要だと思っています。厳選した仕組によりこれを実施しています。さまざまな方法、例えばスポーツやトーク活動などを通じリーダーシップを養成しています。また、企業の社会的責任など高度の職責に関するコースなども設けています。　モチベーションに関しては、主に2つの異なるレベルで指導しています。個人を成長させることと自身を知ることです。これはコーチングであり、メンターです。これは非常に重要な要素です。また、職業プロジェクトがあり、学生は実践的かつ自身に相応しいプロジェクトを選択するか、あるいは自身で新たに考案します。

　複数の専門領域にまたがる教育研究は表面的な知識の修得にとどまってしまう危険な場合もあるとのご意見は、全くそのとおりだと思います。しかし、最も重要なことは、その教育のあと10％程度の学生がそのモチベーションを高めている事実です。

　最後に、この時代に特有な3つの主要キーワードについてお話しします。1つ目は複数の専門領域にまたがる教育研究です。我々にとって非常に重要な2つ目のキーワードはコラボレーションです。共同プロジェクトはむしろ最近の事象です。我々は今まで1つの組織のなかで単独で研究する環境に親しんできましたが、特に欧州でコラボレーションの動きが出てきたため、欧州プロジェクトがどのように機能するかについての話

representative to the way we have to work in companies, for example. The third one is transition. We believe that many people nowadays think that things are rapidly changing, and we believe that it is very important for us to teach our students that nowadays we are in a world of transition. We will not reach some steady states, and we have to work in the transition world, that's my viewpoint that I present.

Zoran Petrović

I had a much broader scope in mind, but I will just address two issues. There was a talk especially by President Tan about these leaders which are needed in well developed countries. To maintain their quality of life with aging society need a large number of engineers and specialists from other countries to maintain their research and productivity and those usually come from not so well developed countries, and those countries always complain about the brain drain, but I do not believe that the brain drain happens when the young people goes from Serbia to United States. It happens when Serbia has a good and high quality position and does not have a qualified person to fill that position because such people have left the country, and you should also specifically look at three types of immigrants or emigrants whatever you prefer, not so well qualified and you need them to conquer some sort of boundaries, new realms like Australia, Canada, or Siberia, or something and then you need a lot of engineers to run processes, but you get this 5%-10% of leaders and there is huge competition to attract those.

合いを行っています。この欧州プロジェクトは日本のJSPS（日本学術振興会）のような仕組で、欧州レベルで異なった機関の間で、異なったカルチャーのもとで、いくつもの共同プロジェクトを実現していかなければなりません。このコラボレーションは、我々が企業で仕事をする際の手本となるでしょう。3つ目のキーワードは転換です。今日、人々は多かれ少なかれ物事が急速に変わりつつあると感じているからです。世界は今転換期にあると学生に教えることは大切なことです。状況はまだ安定に至っておらず、それゆえ、この転換期の中で教育研究をしなければならないのです。以上申し上げたことは私の見解です。

ゾラン ペトロビッチ

　もう少し広い視野での話を考えていたのですが、2点だけ述べることとします。特にタン学長から必要とされるリーダーについてお話がありました。成熟した先進国では社会の高齢化に伴い、その「クオリティー・オブ・ライフ」を維持するために、数多くのエンジニアと専門家を他国から求め、研究と生産性を維持する必要があります。通常、これに応えるのは成熟した先進国出身者とそれ以外からの出身者も多く、そうした国々では常にエンジニアや専門家の頭脳流出を嘆いています。しかし、私は、例えばセルビアから米国に若者が行くことがすなわち頭脳流出であるとは思いません。そうではなく、セルビアに高度な資質をもった人材を受け入れる立派なポジションがあるのに、そのポジションに適した資格を持つ人物が国を去っているがために、そのポジションが埋まらないことが頭脳流出です。また、呼び方は何であれ移民又は移住者には3つのタイプがあります。この3つを分けて考える必要もあります。まずそれほど高い資格を有さない者、これは先進国の労働力不足の限界を克服するために必要とされている人たちです。次いで、オーストラリア、カナダ、あるいはシベリアなどのような新天地に移り住む人たちです。そして、研究や生産のプロセスを動かすために必要とされる多数のエンジニアです。

Fortunately or unfortunately, my country has elitist school system. We take the best 20 students in the whole country and put them in high school which is focused on mathematics and natural sciences and these 20 go to all the Olympiads, score high, bring a lot of medals and let's say 4 years ago Cambridge put out some money and gave them all, this best group in my country, they all get scholarship to go to Cambridge. Before that it was mixed; they will usually go to United States. Actually, a friend of mine who is a professor at Oxford and also at Singapore, double appointment, is now trying to set up a similar scheme at Oxford. So fighting for these 5%, 2%, half a percent leaders is going to be fierce, and universities want them because they need them to run the top level research and stay at universities but also we need them because without them, we will not be able to generate such talented people in future because it is not just genetics, but it is the family attitude which is put into education and put into working habits and attitude towards science which helps generate such people. I will say that we do not suffer brain drain when such people go because we do not have such positions, but we suffer, what we call, the right play, lack of young people that should have been born and nowadays generations of kids going to schools are half in numbers of what they used to be 20 years ago, and I am worried that we will not be able to generate those talented, extra-talented young people.

I will recommend that for some reason, research is usually sort of brought to the countries which have technology but actually it can be exported and actually can be more cost efficient, and I will recommend development of matrix of centers for research in countries which are affiliated associated by a former student of Keio or by a former student of Oxford or Singapore who has his root in not so well developed country to try to maintain their activity or for instance if professor at Keio retires, you can take the equipment there to Vietnam to wherever and continue the research which may

しかし、この5％から10％のリーダーを招請して獲得するためには先進国間であっても激しい競争となります。

　幸か不幸か、セルビアにはエリート養成の教育制度があります。全国から最も優秀な学生20名を選び、数学と自然科学に重点を置く高校で学ばせます。この20名の学生は数学・物理・化学など全科目の国際オリンピックに参加し、優秀な成績を収め、多くのメダルを持ち帰ります。4年前にはケンブリッジ大学が我が国で最も優秀なこのグループ全員に資金を提供し、学生全員がケンブリッジ大学への奨学金を獲得しました。それ以前の進学先はさまざまで、学生の多くは米国の大学に行っていました。私の友人の一人はオックスフォード大学とNUSの教授を兼務しており、この友人がオックスフォード大学でも同様の奨学金の仕組を構築しようと試みています。このように5％、2％、0.5％のリーダーの人材獲得競争は激化しています。大学はこのような人材に大学に残りトップレベルの研究を遂行することを求めているからです。しかし、我が国が彼らを必要とする理由はそれだけではありません。セルビアが将来に向けた才能ある人材を育成する上でも彼らは不可欠な人材だからです。教育に目を向け、学習習慣を身に付けさせ、科学への関心を抱かせるのは遺伝ではなく家庭環境によるものであり、それが才能ある人材の育成につながるからです。我が国の悩みは、適切なポジションがないという理由で優秀な人材が国を去ることによる頭脳流出ではありません。苦しんでいるのは、次代を担う若者の不足です。今日では、就学児童人口は20年前の半分です。我が国は才能ある若者、突出した才能を有する若者を生み出すことができなくなるのではないかと、私は懸念しています。

　私からは次のような提言をさせていただきます。どういう訳か、研究は常に技術を有する国へと持って行かれます。しかし、実際には「研究の輸出」は可能であり、より費用対効果の高いやり方もあります。そこで、私は各国間で研究センターのネットワークを形成することを提言したいと思います。これは慶應義塾大学、オックスフォード大学、NUSなどの卒

be required by Japanese Industry and Japanese Industry may not be able to pay that particular researcher the level of cost of big universities in Japan but may need such research in due course for some applications. So well this is my suggestion.

Arnaud Poitou
This is exactly the reason why we develop branch campuses, just to develop in different places.

Atsushi Seike
Can I just raise another related point about what we are talking, that is sort of basic versus applied, because societies particularly business communities and politics are becoming much and much shortsighted recently. Therefore, most of the research resources or funds are going to the applied research rather than the basic research. But I believe that university should provide the basic research rather than applied research, because business community will be able to do many applied researches, but this is mainly only university that has some independent research institutions which concentrate on this research. The problem is the government subsidies for basic research is now shrinking and, of course, business are not ready to pay much money for the basic research. So maybe only way for us to do that is to provide some of our own funds or to keep asking governments or communities to provide these research funds. Of course, we have to do all kinds of efforts to raise a fund for basic research, but I am just curious to know in what way you are doing?

業生たちが連携、結束し、成熟した先進国ではない国に拠点を置きながら自身の活動を続けるものです。若しくは、例えば慶應義塾大学を退職した教授が研究装置などをベトナムなり他の国へ持って行き、そこで産業界が必要とする可能性がある研究を続けるのです。日本の産業界がこの研究を必要とする際、その研究者に日本の大きな大学と同レベルの費用負担をできないかもしれないからです。しかし、そのような研究が必要とされ、実用化される日が来るかもしれないのです。以上が私からのご提案です。

アルノー ポワトー

これこそが正に、先ほど申し上げたとおり、本学が海外各地で分校を設立している理由です。

清家　篤

今のお話に関連して、別のポイントを挙げたいと思います。基礎対応用の問題です。近年は社会、特に産業界や政治は昔よりはるかに短期的な物の見方をするようになっており、研究資源や資金は基礎研究よりもむしろ応用研究に割り当てられています。しかし、私は大学こそが応用研究よりも基礎研究を提供すべきだと信じています。多くの応用研究は産業界でできるからです。しかし、基礎研究に注力しているのは、大半が大学あるいは独立した研究機関のみです。問題点は、基礎研究に対する政府助成金が縮小しつつあり、当然ながら産業界は基礎研究に多額の資金提供をしようとはしないことです。したがって、我々にできるのは、大学が自ら資金を用意する、あるいは政府や産業界に基礎研究への資金提供をお願いし続けることだけです。もちろん基礎研究資金を調達するために出来る限りのことを実行すべきですが、皆様の大学ではどのようなことをなさっているのでしょうか？

Chorh Chuan Tan

I think it is a very important point that you raised and I don't have the answer, but I can reflect on the things that we have been thinking about. The first is we need to do a better job in articulating how basic research actually leads to societal advantages and improvement. I think just saying that basic research is important is not going to be enough. I think we have to explain much more clearly why and that is the difficult task.

The second is I think we need to work together with the government and industry to create clearer pathways to effective commercialization. In the case of Singapore, we have a strong focus on this. We have research institutes under the Agency for Science Technology and Research which are funded by Ministry of Trade and Industry that are supposed to bridge between universities and industry, and so we are creating much clearer articulations between the university, these institutes and industry. In doing so, we recognize that these articulations vary significantly for different industry sectors such as between ICT and biomedical sciences. From the university's point of view, we must continue to keep a very strong focus on basic research but that cannot be our only goal. We can and should leverage on our strengths to create strong science, health, wealth and/or social impact. In some cases, you could actually contribute to all four. We must show examples of these in order to demonstrate the value of our basic research to the policymakers. This is also why in NUS, we have focused a lot on choosing a limited number of areas where we think we are in a good position to try to create science, health, wealth and social impact. I have one example later which I could share, but I think we have to do this; otherwise, we will not be able to gain the widespread support that we enjoy and which we need to sustain.

第1部　国際学長フォーラム

チョウ チョア タン

　ご指摘の点は大変重要な問題ですが、それに対する答えを私は持ち合わせません。しかし、我々が考えてきたことを改めてしっかりと考えてみましょう。まず1点目ですが、我々は基礎研究がいかに社会の進展や進歩をもたらすかについて、より分かりやすく示す必要があります。基礎研究は重要だと言うだけでは不十分です。その理由をより明確に説明しなければなりません。これはなかなか難しいことです。

　2点目ですが、我々は政府や産業界と協力し、基礎研究を有効に商業ベースに乗せるためのより明確な道筋を構築する必要があると思います。シンガポールでは積極的に、この道筋の構築に努めています。我が国では、産業界と大学との懸け橋となることを企図して、科学技術研究庁（Agency for Science, Technology and Research）傘下に複数の研究機関を設け、貿易産業省（Ministry of Trade and Industry）から資金提供を受けています。これにより、大学、各研究機関、産業界間で明確な連携が図られています。この取組を通じ、これらの連携がICTとバイオメディカルサイエンス間などをはじめとする様々な産業セクターに多大な影響を及ぼすことが分かってきました。大学側の見解を述べると、我々大学は基礎科学への注力を継続する必要はありますが、それが唯一の目標ではありません。大学はその強みを活かし、科学、健康、豊かさ、社会の全て、あるいは、いずれかに大きな影響を及ぼすべきであり、またその力を有しています。大学は今挙げた4項目の全てに、実質的に貢献することもできます。我々大学はこうした事例を提示し、基礎科学の重要性を政策立案者に実証すべきです。シンガポール国立大学はその得意とする領域を絞り、重点的に研究を行ってきたのは、科学、健康、豊かさ、社会に影響を与えることを企図してきたからでもあります。後ほど皆様にご紹介したい本校の事例が1つありますが、今私が述べたようなことを大学で実行しなければなりません。さもなければ、我々が満足し、また持続するために必要な幅広い支援を獲得することはでき

Alison Beale

Again, we don't have the answer to that question but I think in Oxford, we are also finding that the traditional roles that universities have been expected to play are changing very, very rapidly and we happen to be much more open and innovative and change very, very quickly and one of the new kind of roles that people are expecting universities to play are not just generating knowledge and educating students but actually transforming that knowledge into impact and in the UK this idea of impact has been massively important in the last recently particularly with the REF where for the first time, we were asked to demonstrate impact which at first then I think academics felt this was a very difficult task particularly in some subjects. But I think people embraced it very much and it has actually been a way in some instances where certain subjects for example philosophy or other subjects have actually been able to demonstrate how their research actually does have an impact on society. It is one of the new things that recently has had a very big impact on universities in UK.

Fumihiko Kannari

Thank you very much. We discussed the interdisciplinary research and the basic research, and the mutual relation. In my Leading Graduate program, we are getting the assistance from industry and enterprise, and we are chasing the solution with Professors, Students, and Mentors. On the basis of the students who have their big-bone specialty in each of their Gradate school, we certainly treat the real problem in industry or actual society. Always, the interdisciplinary research is required but that is almost the applied research, and on the other hand curiosity-driven basic research is completely outside. That is again the tradeoff between basic

ないでしょう。

アリソン ビール

　タン学長と同様、先ほどの問いかけに対する答えはありません。しかし、オックスフォードでも大学に求められてきた伝統的役割が極めて急速に変わりつつあると感じています。時を同じくして、本学はより革新的で開かれた大学へと、急速な変化を遂げています。人々が大学に期待する新しい役割の1つは、知識の創出と学生の教育だけでなく、その知識を、「実際に影響（impact）を及ぼす形」へと変化させることです。英国ではこのIMPACTという考え方が近年非常に重要となり、特に研究評価（Research Excellence Framework: REF）において重視されています。このたび大学はREFから初めてこのIMPACTを提示するよう求められました。教職員はこの作業に大変苦労し、学部や学科によっては特に困難な作業となりました。とはいえ、皆これを喜んで受け入れていたと思います。実際、例えば哲学などの科目にとってその科目での研究が社会にどのように影響を及ぼすかを提示する手段の1つとなったと思います。以上が、近年英国の大学に非常に大きな影響を与えた新たな動きです。

神成文彦

　どうもありがとうございます。我々は学際研究と基礎研究、また、両者のあるべき関係について討論してまいりました。慶應義塾大学の博士課程教育リーディングプログラムでは産業界の支援を得て、解決策を追求しています。本プログラムではもちろん、大学院生が骨太の専門性をそれぞれの研究科で身に着けると同時に、産業界で実際に生じている問題や実社会の問題を扱っています。学際的研究は常に求められていますが、その大半は分野融合というよりも応用研究で、一方、好奇心に端を発した基礎研究は完全に対象外です。先ほども出ましたが、これが

research and interdisciplinary applied-research. At present, we have to shift the balance or still study the basic research under the requirement of interdisciplinary activity?.

Atsushi Seike
I think two things do not necessarily addressed completely. I mean, of course, you know, every applied research is derived from basic research, and also if you have some interdisciplinary research and apply to solve the problem, then maybe you can find some issues that need to be done in each expertise. I think there will be some feedback from the interdisciplinary research to each field of expertise. It is not necessary that the application is correct one, but our question is, somehow the government and business are focused on the applied research. So what do we have discussed is maybe we need to let people, particularly government and business understand that there is a clear relation or bridge between basic and applied science.

Toshiaki Makabe
I have a chance to say something. It is very impressive for your discussion as for interdisciplinary researches. I think this kind of interdisciplinary field will be further developed based on the academic fusion or renovation of the traditional research field. University or institution should foster very strong young students under these circumstances. Of course, all the presidents cultivate such kind of young people under these circumstances in the academia. What do you think, President Seike?

Atsushi Seike
Yes, it is very demanding as a manager making the bridge between the basic research and application or the interdisciplinary research.

基礎研究と学際的応用研究とのトレードオフの問題です。我々大学はこのバランスを変える必要があるのでしょうか、あるいは学際的研究が求められる中で依然として基礎研究に軸を置くべきなのでしょうか？

清家　篤

この2つは必ずしも、完全に相反するものではないと思います。つまり、全ての応用研究は基礎研究から発していることは、もちろん皆様ご承知のことです。また、問題解決に学際的応用研究を用いた場合でも、おそらく、各専門領域での研究を必要とする問題が生じることでしょう。私は、学際的研究から各専門領域に対して何らかのフィードバックがなされると思っています。応用研究だけが正解とする必要はありません。しかし、問題は、ともかく政府や産業界などが応用研究を重視していることです。したがって、我々が話し合うべきは、基礎研究と応用研究の間には明確な関連又はつながりがあることを、特に政府や産業界の人々に対し知らしめる必要があるということです。

真壁利明

一言発言させていただきます。学際的領域に関する大変素晴らしい議論が進められておりますが、このような学際領域の発展には既存の学問体系の融合、あるいは研究領域の組み換え刷新がもととなるでしょう。我々慶應義塾大学をはじめ大学では、社会的に大きな影響力のある人物をこのような環境のもとで育成しなければならないと考えています。もちろんご出席の学長方の教育研究機関においてはそのような環境を実現していると思います。清家塾長、ご意見を伺えますか？

清家　篤

そうですね。基礎研究と応用を結び付けること、あるいは学際的研究を実施することがマネージャーに強く求められているのは確かです。非

Definitely it is very important, but usually I need Ph.D. students just to do science and making the good establishment, not as the manager. So maybe that is one of the aim of the establishment of our Lead-
ing Graduate School program. Are there any particular educational systems to educate such kind of generalist taking care of the full research area and making a bridge between industrial and academic research?

Arnaud Poitou
I think I already mentioned the points. I am very sensitive to President Tan, speaking about the ecosystem. This is a point and it is really important, and we try to develop that. Concerning your question, I really believe that everything is not a question of know-how. Beside that, especially if you want to have a researcher who can also be a good manager, it is not only a question of know-how, it is a question of interpersonal skill and motivation. This is difficult to know how we educate students in that direction, but we believe that we have to try to do it probably through mentor's coaching experiences, development of interpersonal things, mixing students together, giving them the experience to go abroad, and so on. These few types of interpersonal skills can lead them to develop the ability to manage, besides the precise scientific competence. I think it is not a question of know-how.

Chorh Chuan Tan
Well, I have two thoughts on the question from participant. One is

常に重要なことです。しかし、私は、博士課程の学生にはきちんと科学を学び、確固とした骨太の基礎を確立することを求めています。単なるマネージャーではないのですから。大学院学生が骨太の専門性をもつことは本学の博士課程リーディングプログラムの目的の1つでしょう。皆様の大学では、何か特別なジェネラリスト教育制度、つまり研究領域についての十分な指導を行いながら、かつ、産業界で必要とされる研究と学術研究とをつなげるような教育の仕組みはありますか。

アルノー ポワトー

　ジェネラリスト教育については先ほどご説明しましたが、その前に、私はエコシステムについてのタン学長のお話に大いに共感します。この点は極めて重要であり、我々はその構築に向けて努めるべきです。清家塾長のご質問についてですが、ノウハウの問題だけではないと思います。ノウハウの問題以外にも、特に、研究員であると同時に優れたマネージャーでもある人物を育成しようとする場合、それは対人スキルやモチベーションの問題でもあります。このような方向へと学生を指導する方法を見つけることは大変難しいことですが、本校ではメンターとしてのコーチング経験、対人スキルの育成、混成学生集団、海外経験の提供などの方法を通じ、それを目指すべきであると思っています。学生がこうした対人スキルの型をいくつか身に付けることにより、科学に関する確実な能力の他に、今後の人生で用いるマネジメント力の習得にもつなげることができます。これはノウハウの問題ではないと思います。

チョウ チョア タン

　ご出席の方のご質問に対し、2つコメントがあります。1点目は教育に

related to the question on education. As Professor Poitou says, I think know-how for students is not a new problem. Interpersonal skills are very important, but there are a range of ways we can help our students to develop these; but I think the motivation part is the really critical one. In our case, we focus a lot on what we call entrepreneurship. This does not just refer to graduates having successful start-up companies and all that. It is also about how we can help our students become more entrepreneurial in their thinking, to be willing and able to seize opportunities to create value. This is how we define "being entrepreneurial". The flagship program in NUS for this is our unique NUS Overseas College program. NOC attracts some of the most entrepreneurial students from Singapore and around Asia, and then they have a very special experiential entrepreneurship educational experience. The alumni from this program have been very successful, for eg in creating more than 200 start-up companies. Again, NOC only involves less than 5% the NUS undergraduate population, but we think it is enough to drive the broader student culture. I think in the longer term, we need more and more graduates who are enterprising in their thinking.

Coming to the issue of academic leaders, it is very important that they are respected for their academic ability and standing, but in my own experience, actually some of the people who are best at research are not really good at administration. In our universities, there are always a few people who despite big difficulties, are able create an outstanding new center or a top-quality program, against the odds. When we find somebody like that, try our best to support them, perhaps reduce the teaching load, help them become more competitive because that is the best way to discover and develop these individuals, people who get things done well. Often they are strong researchers but sometimes, they are competent researchers who have enough academic stripes to justify being a leader, but have a great ability to recruit and nurture faculty who are stronger

関するものです。ポワトー校長がおっしゃったとおり、学生にノウハウを教えることは新しい命題ではありません。対人スキルは非常に重要であり、学生の対人スキルを伸ばすには様々な方法があります。しかし、モチベーションは極めて重要です。本学の場合、我々がアントレプレナーシップ（起業家精神）と称するものを極めて重視しています。この言葉は、卒業生が起業に成功するようなことのみを指すのではありません。学生のアントレプレナー的発想をいかに育み、また、価値創造の機会を躊躇せずに捕え、その機会を捕える能力をいかに習得させるか、を指しています。これが本学における「アントレプレナーであること」の定義です。このアントレプレナーシップを象徴するNUSのプログラムが、本学独自の海外カレッジプログラム（Overseas College Program）です。本プログラムには、シンガポールやアジア各国から最もアントレプレナーシップ溢れる学生が集まってきています。ここで学生たちは、特別かつ実践的なアントレプレナーシップ学習を経験します。本プログラム修了者は成功を収めており、例えば彼らが創設した企業数は200以上に上ります。繰り返しになりますが、海外カレッジプログラム履修者数は、NUS全学部学生の5％にも満たないものですが、校風の多様化を推し進めるには十分な数です。長期的には、事業的観点から思考する卒業生を増やす必要があると思います。

次いで教員のリーダーについてですが、このリーダーがその見識や地位の高さから尊敬を得ることは非常に重要だと思います。しかし私の経験から申し上げると、実際には、研究では最高の成果をあげる者が、管理能力においては十分な成果をあげない場合も見受けられます。本学には、どのような大きな困難があろうとも大方の予想を裏切り、画期的なセンターを創設し、あるいは抜群のプログラムを考案する人物が、常に数名在籍しています。このような人物を見出した場合は、その人物を援助するために最善を尽すことです。例えば指導に要する負担を減らし、その人物がより能力を発揮するよう便宜を図ります。これがこのような人

researchers or teachers than themselves. Such individuals can be highly effective leaders even though they may not be the strongest researcher in the Faculty.

Closing

Fumihiko Kannari
We have been sharing a very stimulating discussion. It is a good time to close the forum. I'd like to ask President Seike to have the concluding remark.

Atsushi Seike
I would like to say again thank you so much. I deeply appreciate your participation, and I enjoyed the discussion as well and I hope you too have enjoyed the discussion. Thank you very much.

Toshiaki Makabe
As a forum organizer, I satisfy today's International Presidents Forum. The discussion is very deep and the mutual understanding will be very essential for our near future direction of university or academia. Judging from the great success of today's forum, I would like to propose the second Forum in next spring or so. Your opinion about the second forum and the suggestion will be very helpful for us. We are very grateful to open the second. Your continued contribution to and cooperation with Keio university will be also appreciated.

物、つまり優れた成果を残す人物を発見し、育成する最良の方法だからです。このような人物は往々にして優秀な研究員でもあります。のみならず、リーダーの地位を正当化するに足る学術的系統を備えた有能な研究者であり、また自分より優秀な研究員や教員を集めて育成する能力に長けた人物である場合もあります。このような人物は、教員の中の最も優秀な研究者ではないかもしれませんが、影響力の大きいリーダーとなり得るのです。

終わりに

神成文彦

大変有意義な討論でしたが、そろそろ閉会にしたいと存じます。清家塾長に締めの挨拶をお願いします。

清家　篤

改めまして皆様にお礼申し上げます。ご参加いただきましたことに心より感謝いたします。大変有意義な議論を堪能しました。皆様にとってもそうであったことを願います。どうもありがとうございました。

真壁利明

本フォーラムのオーガナイザーとして1つご提案があります。本日は深く掘り下げた本当に有意義な議論がなされました。フォーラムのこの大成功を受け、来春を目途に第2回国際学長フォーラムを開催することをご提案したいと思います。第2回フォーラムに関するご意見や、開催候補地、開催月についてのご提案があれば、ぜひお知らせください。第2回フォーラム開催に関しては柔軟に対応させていただきます。その際はご協力のほどよろしくお願いいたします。

Fumihiko Kannari

It seems all of you agree on this. Thank you very much for your participation in today's International Presidents Forum, and I really appreciate your kind cooperation. *Arigatou gozaimasu.*

神成文彦

　ただ今の提案に皆様ご賛成いただけるようです。それでは、本日この国際学長フォーラムにご出席いただき誠にありがとうございました。皆様のご協力に心より感謝いたします。

Part 2　第2部

Keio, Five-year Program for Leading Graduate School
慶應義塾、5年一貫リーディング大学院プログラム

Chapter 1
Essays Presented by Leaders

1. OPENING OF KEIO'S PROGRAM

1.1
On the launch of the Science for Development of Super Mature Society Program

Professor
Atsushi SEIKE
President, Keio University

The population of Japan is aging at a globally unprecedented pace. The proportion of older people is increasing while the total population is gradually decreasing, a trend that may cause economic and general social malaise. The oft-expressed sense of social stagnation in Japan may also be related to these changes in the population demographics.

These problems affect not only Japan but also other developed countries which are experiencing the same aging populations now. In time, it may also become a problem affecting those developing countries which will face aging populations sooner or later.

In this 'super mature society', quantitative expansion alone will not allow for the continued development of the economic society. Instead, we must aim for development through an increase in quality, in particular an increase in the quality of life. Japan has the difficult task of constructing a mature society – moreover a super mature society – in the positive sense, and the best efforts

第1章
リーディング大学院プログラムに寄せて

1. プログラム開設にあたって

1.1 超成熟社会発展のサイエンスプログラムの開始にあたって

清家 篤　慶應義塾長

　日本はいま世界に類を見ない高齢化を経験しつつあります。これは総人口が減少しつつ高齢者の割合は増加するという現象で、経済や社会全般の停滞を引き起こす原因ともなります。よく言われる社会の閉塞感もこれと無関係ではないでしょう。

　こうした現象は日本だけでなく同じように高齢化しつつある他の先進国にも共通の問題です。またやがては同じように高齢化する発展途上国にも起こりうる問題でもあります。

　このような超成熟社会というべき状況の下では、量的拡大のみによる経済社会の持続的発展は望めません。そこではむしろ、質の高度化、特に生活の質の高度化による発展を目指すべきです。良い意味での成熟社会、さらには超成熟社会の構築ということで、日本は今、この難問に直面して懸命にその解を求めているところです。そして日本がその解を見つければ、同じような問題を抱える先進国に良きモデルを提供できますし、また遅かれ早かれ同じような問題に直面する発展途上国にも大いに参考

are being made to devise a solution. If Japan can find the answers, it can provide a good model for other developed countries experiencing the same kinds of issues, and this model will also be an important reference for developing countries that come to face the same problems in the future.

There are increasingly higher expectations for universities to create a vision for this new super mature society through academic study and research. The 'Science for Development of Super Mature Society' program, proposed by Keio and selected as one of the Leading Graduate School Programs (all-round type) last year, is designed to meet these expectations.

This five-year graduate program, which integrates elements of both the sciences and humanities, is an ambitious project to cultivate leaders who will guide new and sustained development in the coming era. The curriculum incorporates a variety of aspiring ideas which are quite new for graduate school programs, such as classes and lectures, in which students work together with industry and government to find solutions to various current social issues.

We greatly appreciate your encouragement of the participating students and support of Keio's new challenges.

(2012 June)

1. プログラム開設にあたって

になるでしょう。

　そしてそうした超成熟社会の新たな姿を学問によって示す大学への期待はますます大きくなっています。慶應義塾が博士課程教育リーディングプログラム（オールラウンド型）に昨年提案し、採択された「超成熟社会発展のサイエンス」は、そうした期待に応えるための設計となっています。

　5 年一貫の文理融合を基本とした大学院教育を通じて次の時代の新しい持続的な発展の先頭に立つ先導力を養成する野心的なプログラムです。今日の社会の諸問題の解決策を産官と一緒になって取り組む授業等、数々の意欲的な試みがカリキュラムとして組まれており、従来の大学院教育にない内容となっています。

　このプログラムに参加している学生たちへの激励と、慶應義塾の取り組みへのご支援を、心よりお願いする次第です。

（2012 年 6 月）

1. OPENING OF KEIO'S PROGRAM

1.2
BasicPhilosophy Guiding the Science Program for Development of Super Mature Society

Professor
Kouhei OHNISHI
Program Coordinator

The time will soon come when developmental plateaus of a super mature society are fully established. Human kind has never experienced this before. To continue to flourish in the 21st century as a super mature society, we will need ingenious leaders in all of its segments. These new leaders will face daunting challenges. Perhaps, the most significant challenge is that the industrial structure which accomplished standardized mass production in the 20th century for the purpose of economic growth must re-organize itself. Now, QoL or Quality of Life is the primary need. Building a new industrial structure will require new kinds of leaders who possess not only a high level of specialization but also exposure to and expertise in engineering, policy planning, social management and medical sciences. To date there has been no formal effort to cultivate this new brand of leaders despite the fact that every segment of politics, business and society has been searching for these leaders. The Keio program fills this role.

Focused on Science for Development of a Super Mature Society, the leading graduate school program was implemented to develop the leadership traits just described in a five-year MMD system (double master "MM" and single doctoral "D" programs). The first master program involves the student's primary

1. プログラム開設にあたって

1.2 超成熟社会発展の サイエンスプログラムの 基本方針

大西公平 プログラムコーディネーター、理工学部教授

　もうまもなく、これまで人類が経験したことのない超成熟社会が実現しようとしている。21世紀の世界でこの超成熟社会を発展させるためには、社会の様々な断面で独創的な指導者が必要になる。たとえば、標準化による大量生産を目指す20世紀型産業構造は高いQoLを目指す新しい社会潮流の中でその構造自体を変えていかねばならない。新しい産業構造を作るためには、工学的側面、政策・社会学的側面、医療学的側面のそれぞれの専門家だけではなく、深い専門力と広い俯瞰力を兼ね備えた指導者が必要である。このような指導者は政治、経済、社会のあらゆる分野で求められているにもかかわらず、これまで積極的かつ組織的に育成する努力が不足していた。

　博士課程教育プログラム「超成熟社会発展のサイエンス」は5年一貫で、修士ダブルディグリーシステムと博士号を取得する中で、深い専門力と広い俯瞰力を獲得するプログラムである。

　最初の修士課程では思考の武器となる高い専門性を獲得する。続いて、異なる専門に移り、社会の様々な問題点を洗い出し経験するグループプロジェクト演習を中心とする第二の修士課程を経る。この二つの修士号取得により高いレベルにおける文理融合を行うとともに、超成熟社会を発展させるための課題を抽出し、それをサイエンスとして解決し、博士号を

specialization. The second master program involves complementary disciplines targeting a broadening of the student's knowledge. A series of group project exercises extends throughout the program providing exposure to actual societal issues. A doctoral degree will be conferred after a project on the science for the development of a super mature society is successfully completed.

The entire five-year MMD graduate program has a unique and well thought through a core curriculum. To provide a strong perspective in a wide variety of fields pertinent to society's challenges, all enrolled graduate students, whether a humanity or science major, are required to take the core curriculum and the secondary curriculum of science and technology, media and governance and medicine. The program has also set up an opportunity for students to improve their communication and negotiation skills in English, a skill essential for involvement on the global stage.

The only requirement for admission of any graduate students to the present program is to enroll one of thirteen general graduate programs. Of these graduate students, candidates for the present program will be competitively selected and hired as a research assistant (RA). All RAs will be on a stipend. A further unique aspect of the program is that the detailed plan for participation in the five-year program will be a decision of students. There is no pre-set path. Guidance and/or advice from members of the program committee and mentors facilitate their decision. The program was designed in such a way that each student can choose his or her own career path based on his/her personality, motivation and needs. In this sense, the present program is designed to be both semi-autonomous (student-centric) and collaborative being supported by the highly innovative community (community-based) of Keio University.

(2012 August)

取得する。この5年の課程をMMD方式と呼んでいる。MMD方式が有効に働くためには、カリキュラム構成が重要である。本プログラムでは、俯瞰力を高めるため、文理の区別なく全員が履修をするコアカリキュラムと理工、政策社会、医療の3専門分野において履修すべき科目を定めている。また、将来の国際社会での活躍を念頭に置き、英語によるコミュニケーション力や交渉力を訓練する場も設けてある。

このプログラムに参加する大学院生は既に慶應義塾大学大学院13研究科に在籍していることのみが条件になっており、その中から競争的に選抜され、リサーチアシスタント（RA）として雇用される。RAには給与が支給される。しかし、プログラムの参加の仕方は決まりきった内容ではない。むしろ、5年間をどのように使うかという点について個人の自由に任されている。もちろん、プログラム委員会やメンターによる助言やアドバイスがさらに有効に働く。これは、各自のキャリアパスが十人十色であり、それぞれの個性を生かすようなプログラムが構成できるようになっているからである。

この意味で本プログラムはRAの自発性を重んじるプログラムであると同時に、慶應義塾大学大学院全体が支援する画期的なプログラムなのである。

（2012年8月）

1. OPENING OF KEIO'S PROGRAM

1.3
Close Encounters of the Third Kind

Professor
Akira HASEYAMA
Vice-President, Keio University
Program Supervisor

The Keio Leading Graduate School Program for "the Science for Development of Super Mature Society" has commenced its activities. Although there was only a short time between its actual selection and kick-off dates, graduate students of the Leading Program have already been fully engaged as Research Assistants (RAs) through the first semester of 2012. At the home of the program, Hiyoshi Campus West Annex, spirited discussions and heated debates are a regular occurrence among the student RAs, faculty and mentors from industry and government. Such a successful start was accomplished during our busiest period, the end of the 2011 school and fiscal year. This was the result of extraordinary efforts made by all members of the program. Here, I would like to express my sincere gratitude for their extraordinary efforts, particularly to the program coordinator Prof. Kouhei OHNISHI (Faculty of Science and Technology), the chief curriculum coordinator Prof. Fumihiko KANNARI (Chair of Graduate Education Committee, Faculty of Science and Technology) and the founder and chairman of board council of the program Prof. Toshiaki MAKABE (Vice-President of Keio University).

As implemented by the Ministry of Education, Culture, Sports, Science and Technology of Japanese Government, the Program

1. プログラム開設にあたって

1.3
「未知との遭遇」がはじまった?

長谷山彰　慶應義塾　常任理事　プログラム責任者

　慶應義塾リーディング大学院プログラム「超成熟社会発展のサイエンス」が走り出した。プログラムの採択から開始まで極めて短い期間しかなかったが、既に初年度から大学院生をRAとして採用して本格的な活動が始まっている。本拠地である日吉キャンパス西別館では、産学官から参加したメンターを交えて、白熱した議論のある授業を展開している。年度末の学事繁忙の時期にここまで漕ぎ着けることができたのは関係者の並々ならぬご努力の賜物である。特にプログラムコーディネーターの大西公平理工学部教授、理工学研究科学習指導主任・プログラム運営委員として学事面の調整にご苦労頂いた神成文彦教授、そしてリーディング大学院プログラムの生みの親ともいうべきボード会議議長の真壁利明常任理事のご尽力は多大である。紙上を借りて感謝を捧げたい。

　文科省が公募した博士課程教育リーディングプログラムは、産学官の連携によって、俯瞰力と独創力を備え、産学官にわたってグローバルに活躍できるリーダーを養成することを要求していた。

　義塾のこのプログラムも5年一貫の文理融合を基本とした大学院教育を通じて、超成熟社会という前例のない時代に、その持続的発展の先頭に立つリーダーを養成することを目標に掲げている。総人口の減少と高齢者の割合増加という事態はこれまで世界のどの国も経験したことがな

for Leading Graduate Schools requires development of global leaders who can bring deep insights, original solutions and a grasp of the "big picture" of societal issues, to their roles in academia, industry and government. Through a five-year graduate program which integrates both sciences and humanities, the Keio Leading Graduate School Program has as a goal to develop leaders at the forefront of sustainable development, particularly in this unprecedented era of the super mature society. We, as a society, and our new leaders are facing the "unknown." No single nation in the world has encountered the present situation of a decline of the total population coincident with an increasing aged population.

Low birthrate, increasing longevity and globalization along with the Great East Japan Earthquake all made our lives and future uncertain. Now more than ever, enveloped in uncertainty, we need leaders with vision, a global mindset and the strength to execute on their ideas. The concept of the ideal leader is elusive as what constitutes a good leader has varied geographically and through history. Future global leaders must be mindful of the fine line between leadership and authoritarianism, as history has often seen societies 'hope in individual leaders' transition to a witnessing of calamity. We need to cultivate intelligent and capable leaders who can not only lead people but be one with the people as well.

Globalization has made close contacts among different cultures routine. This is another way we face the "unknown." People's reactions vary when they encounter the unknown. Reactions may be aggressive behavior driven by vigilance or compliant behavior motivated by avoidance. To cope with the "unknown", ideally society and its leaders should be able to perceive the fact over emotion and stereotype and to seek out constructive solution (s) by employing a persevering and multifaceted way of thinking. More than the analytic, soft skills such as the ability to understand others and effectively negotiate are imperative as society's problems inherently involve people. Although it is quite difficult to cultivate

1. プログラム開設にあたって

いという意味で、未知との遭遇と呼べる。

　少子高齢化、グローバル化に加えて東日本大震災後の先行きに対する不透明感が相俟って、ビジョンを示して強力に社会を牽引できるリーダーの登場が待望されている。世界で戦える人材をという声も聞こえる。しかし、リーダー像というものは時代によって国によってまちまちであり、理想のリーダー像を示すことは難しい。民衆の待望の内に登場したリーダーが結局は独裁者として民族に惨禍をもたらした事例は歴史上枚挙に暇がない。リードすることリードされることの双方において賢明な人材を育成することが真のリーダーを生み出す要件である。

　グローバル化によって異文化との接触も増えている。未知との遭遇に直面して人間が示す反応は色々である。警戒心から来る攻撃的反応、とりあえず争いを回避する迎合的態度などさまざまであろう。過去に経験したことのない事態に対応するためには、まず事態の本質を見抜いた上で、感情まかせの短絡的思考に陥らず、粘り強い多面的な思考に基づいて、創造的な解決法を生み出す必要がある。相手のある話であれば理解力や交渉力も必要になろう。こうした総合力を備えた人材を学校教育によって生み出すことはなかなか難しいが、慶應義塾は長い年月、そうした人材の育成に努めてきた。世の流行に惑わされず、物事の本質を見抜き、正しいことを信念を持って実行する独立自尊の人材育成である。独裁的なリーダーや国家機構に頼るのではなく、学問を修め、生業を持ち、加えて、自らがあたかも総理大臣や外務大臣や大蔵大臣であるかのような心持ちで国や社会の行く末を主体的に考えることのできる市民を多く育成することが真の近代化につながるという福沢諭吉の信念に基づいている。

　深い専門と幅広い教養を身につけ、強靭な思考力と創造力、異文化を理解するコミュニケーション能力と互いの主張の違いを克服できる交渉力を備えた人材は狭い専門分野に特化した教育、教室の中での座学だけでは生み出すことができない。リーディング大学院が掲げる教育、すなわ

through a university education the soft and hard skills needed in its leaders by the super mature society, Keio University has been making tremendous efforts to cultivate these types of people for such a long time. As a university community we have sought to cultivate students having a spirit of independence and self-respect paired with the ability to perceive the fact and carry out a correct path with their faith, not being confused by world trends. It was the belief of our founder Yukichi FUKUZAWA that modernization does not evolve through autocratic leaders or governmental organizations. True modernization, he asserted, may only be accomplished by cultivating citizens who are academically trained, carry knowledge into an occupation, and are capable of thinking proactively about the future fate of society and country as if they themselves were the prime minister, minister of foreign affairs or minister of finance.

People with deep expertise, a broad range of knowledge, strong thoughts and originality, communication skills to understand different cultures and negotiation skills to overcome contentious issues cannot be cultivated within specialized fields of education and inside classes alone. Our Leading Graduate School Program strives to grow leaders through education in both sciences and humanities where both disciplines necessarily intersect, through cross communication opportunities with experts representing a wide range of different sectors of society and finally by study abroad.

Following our tradition at Keio University, I have a great hope that our Leading Graduate School Program will strive for further progress.

(2012 September)

1. プログラム開設にあたって

ち文理融合、分野横断型の学習、社会の幅広い分野の専門家との交流を含む体験的学習、海外での学習経験などによって初めて可能になる。

　義塾の伝統を受け継ぎ、さらなる発展をめざすリーディング大学院に大いに期待したい。

（2012 年 9 月）

2. ANTICIPATION OF KEIO'S PROGRAM

2.1
A Bridgehead for a New 'Encouragement of Learning'

Professor
Kan SUZUKI
Keio University, Former Senior Vice Minister of the Ministry of Education, Culture, Sports, Science and Technology - Japan

During my service as the Senior Vice Minister of the Japanese Ministry of Education, Culture, Sports, Science and Technology (MEXT), I encountered a strong feeling of discontentment within our universities. To address this issue and to revitalize our deeply entrenched commitment to academia, I formulated the blueprint for the Program for Leading Graduate Schools (PLGS). A key aspect of the blueprint was the concept of the All-Round type of the PLGS.

Prior to my appointment as the Senior Vice-Minister, I conceived the policy described by the phrase, "From Concrete to People." At the time of my appointment, the situation in universities was not good. The national budget for universities had not been increased for ten years. It was perceived that the increase of the budget had not been agreed to or approved by the public. Moreover, top business and industry executives proclaimed, 'We do not expect anything from universities.' Responsible for university budgets and recognizing the need for their increase, I felt a sense of crisis. Rather than surrender to this sentiment, I responded to the challenge by formulating a blueprint for change. Keio University was first to stand by me, responding to the challenge by 'Building a center for excellence to meet our commitment to academia.'

2. プログラムへの期待

2.1
新たな「学問のすゝめ」の橋頭保に

鈴木　寛　慶應義塾大学教授・元文部科学副大臣

　私が、文部科学副大臣在任中に、リーディング大学院という構想を考案させていただいた。特にオールラウンド型については、日本社会に渦巻く大学への不信を一掃し、学問を重んずる風土を再び日本に取り戻すための橋頭堡を造るとの強い思いで提案した。

　「コンクリートから人へ」を掲げて私が文部科学副大臣に就任するまで、大学予算マイナスが十年近く続いた。大学予算拡充策は、国内世論から低い理解と支持しか得られなかったからだ。経済界の重鎮までもが「大学には何も期待しない」と豪語していた。大学予算増の先頭に立った私は、四面楚歌。このときの悔しさと危機感から、すべては始まった。「学問を修め・究めることの意義を再び天下に示す拠点を造る」との私たちの強い思いに、真っ先に応えていただいたのが「慶應義塾」であった。

　日本経済の復活も「学問」と直結している。日本企業は、連続的な改良には強いが、非連続なイノベーションに弱い。新たなパラダイムを切り拓き、新規のプロジェクトをどんどん立ち上げていくためにも、原理・原則・基礎・基本を徹底的に修めた上での跳躍。まさに、学問が不可欠だ。

　日本企業に博士号取得者が少ないために、海外での商機もみすみす失っている。米国では人事部長の7割が修士・博士、日本では役員クラスですら5％に満たない。日本は、米・英・仏・韓国などに比べても、人

2. ANTICIPATION OF KEIO'S PROGRAM

Japan is entering a new era. Revitalization of the Japanese economy is directly associated with the state of academia. Japanese enterprises excel at continuous improvement, but not at discontinuous innovation. The seeds of innovation are rooted in a foundation of fundamental principles and basic learning. Therefore, a new paradigm is needed in academia to revitalize our economy. Understanding this point is made clear by looking at data. Nearly 70% of personnel directors in US companies are master (M.S.) and/or doctoral (Ph.D.) degree-holders, whereas only 5% of the same executives in Japanese companies hold the same degree. In addition, as compared to those in the US, UK, France and South Korea, a relative ratio of graduate school students per population is very low. Due to a lack of people with Ph.D. in Japan, business opportunities are at risk of being lost abroad. Cultivating competent leaders with Ph.D. is of strategic importance to Japan.

By cultivating leaders for the new era, the Keio PLGS will demonstrate the potential that academia has to positively impact our society. As a newly appointed faculty member of Keio University, I promise a deep commitment to this challenge.

(2014 March)

2. プログラムへの期待

口あたりの大学院生比率が極端に低い。博士号をもち、真に実力のある社会リーダーの養成が急務である。

　リーディング大学院から、社会変革のリーダー、新時代の先導者が、続々と輩出され、学問の大切さや可能性を、天下に見せつけてほしい。このたび塾の一員に加えていただいた私も、全力を尽くしたい。

（2014 年 3 月）

2. ANTICIPATION OF KEIO'S PROGRAM

2.2
Great Expectations for Keio's New Program

Professor
Roger GOODMAN
University of Oxford

Japan of course is not the only advanced country in the world which is ageing fast, but it is almost certainly the country which is most aware of the speed of its demographic transition and the effect that this will have on every aspect of social and economic policy over the next twenty-five years. It is, therefore, a huge and deserved credit to Keio University that it has chosen "Science for Development of Super Mature Society" as the main theme for the newly established Leading Graduate School Program. I, personally, am very much looking forward to working with colleagues at Keio through this programme: first, as an anthropologist of Japanese society who has spent many years examining the effects of Japan's changing demography, and second as Head (Dean) of Social Sciences at the University of Oxford, which has also embarked on innovative new graduate programmes of its own in recent years to confront major global social issues such as ageing.

The dramatic demographic shift which is taking place in Japan as it becomes a super mature society has generally been talked about in terms of constituting a 'national crisis'. There is room, however, for a more positive view. Japan's older population is an affluent one; the current generation of retirees, especially those who retired from government service or from large companies,

2. プログラムへの期待

2.2
慶應の新プログラムに対する Oxford からの期待

ロジャー グッドマン　オックスフォード大学教授、
社会科学部長、ニッサン・プロフェッサー

　日本が急速に高齢化している唯一の先進国でないことは言うまでもありません。しかし、人口高齢化の変化のスピードと、それが今後25年間に社会及び経済政策のあらゆる面にもたらす影響について、最も認識している国が日本であることは間違いありません。その意味で、慶應義塾大学が新しく発足したリーディング大学院プログラムの主要テーマとして「超成熟社会発展のサイエンス」を取り上げたことは、称賛に値する大きな意義を有していると思います。私自身は、このプログラムを通じて慶應の皆さんと協力していくことを楽しみにしています。一つはこれまで長年にわたって人口構造の変化が日本社会にもたらす影響を分析してきた文化人類学者としてですが、もう一つは、最近、高齢化のような世界的な社会問題に対応するための独自の革新的な大学院プログラムを立ち上げたオックスフォード大学の社会科学部長としてでもあります。

　日本が超成熟社会に移行していくなかで起こりつつある人口構造の劇的な変化については、これまで、それが「国家的な危機」をもたらすという意味合いで語られることが一般的でした。しかし、より前向きな捉え方ができるのではないかと考えています。日本の高齢者は豊かです。現在の退職者、特に政府や大企業で働いてきた人は、スカンジナビアを除く世界のどの国よりも高い給付を享受しています。「活動的な高齢者」

enjoy benefits that are better than anywhere else in the world other than Scandinavia. 'Active ageing' is on the rise and many people well into their seventies increasingly contribute directly to the economy. While Japan is a much more mature society than the US, its expenditure on medical care as a proportion of GDP is roughly half, due to a much more efficient system of allocating medical resources. Indeed, I have argued elsewhere that the changing demographic structure in Japan could lead ultimately to a more open, international, egalitarian society with a high quality of life for the population as a whole.

Since many economically advanced societies expect to go down this same demographic path, they will be watching the Japanese case with particular interest. The next generation of Japanese leaders have a huge responsibility to manage this demographic transition and this is why Keio's new programme is so significant. It will require individuals to have a broad knowledge of medicine, science, social science and indeed the arts and humanities to deal with the full complexity of the problems which will face Japan. It is in recognition of these challenges that we have recently established in Oxford the new Blavatnik School of Government (http://www.bsg.ox.ac.uk) which will train future world leaders in all of these disciplines. It is also why all of our research students these days must be fully trained to a high level in both quantitative and qualitative research skills before they can receive their doctoral degrees (http://dtc.socsci.ox.ac.uk). I hope very much that we in Oxford can work with colleagues in Keio as we together try and realise our dream of creating the next generation of genuinely interdisciplinary scholars able to contribute to working on real-life social issues.

Roger Goodman is Nissan Professor of Modern Japanese Studies and Head of the Social Sciences Division, University of Oxford, UK. He has published many books on Japanese education and social policy. His most recent book is with Tuukka Toivonen

2. プログラムへの期待

も増加しており、70歳を優に超えた多くの人たちが経済に直接的な貢献をしています。日本は米国よりもはるかに成熟しているにもかかわらず、日本の医療費をGDP比でみると米国の約半分に止まっており、このことから資源を医療に配分する仕組みがはるかに効率的であることが分かります。別の機会にも論じたように、人口構造の変化を契機に、日本がより開かれた、国際的で平等な社会になり、国民全体が質の高い生活を享受できるようになる可能性があるのです。

多くの先進国が同じような人口構造の変化をたどることが予想されているだけに、日本の事例は特別な注目を集めるでしょう。次代の日本のリーダーたちは、この人口構造の変化に上手に対応する非常に重い責任があります。だからこそ慶應のこの新しいプログラムは重要なのです。日本が直面する複雑な問題に取り組むために、一人ひとりが、医学、自然科学、社会科学、人文科学に関する幅広い知識を持つことが必要になります。このような課題への挑戦が必要だと認識しているからこそ、私たちも、オックスフォードに、ブラヴァトニック・スクール・オブ・ガバメント (http://www.bsg.ox.ac.uk) を新たに設立し、将来の世界的なリーダーたちに、上記の学問の全てにわたってトレーニングを施すことにしました。また、同じ理由から、オックスフォードの大学院生には、博士号を授与する前提として、定量的手法と定性的分析の両面で高度な研究能力を身に付けることを求めるようになっています (http://dtc.socsci.ox.ac.uk)。実生活上の社会問題の解決に貢献できるような、真に学際的な次代の研究者を育てる夢を実現するために、オックスフォードにいる私たちは、慶應の皆さんと力を合わせていければと心より願っています。

ロジャー グッドマン氏は、オックスフォード大学の現代日本研究専攻ニッサン・プロフェッサーで、社会科学部長。日本の教育と社会政策に関する多くの著作があり、近著はトゥーッカ トイボネン（オックスフォード大学）、井本由紀（慶應義塾大学）との共著 A Sociology of Japanese

(Oxford) and Yuki Imoto (Keio University) entitled A Sociology of Japanese Youth (Routledge, 2012) which will be published in Japanese by Akashi Shoten as 『若者問題の社会学―「帰国子女」から「ニート」まで』.

(2012 November)

Youth（Routledge, 2012）で、邦訳版は『若者問題の社会学—「帰国子女」から「ニート」まで』として明石書店より出版予定）。

(2012 年 11 月)

2. ANTICIPATION OF KEIO'S PROGRAM

2.3
Great Hopes in Keio's Challenge: Development Global Leaders from Japan

Takashi KAWAMURA
Chairman of the Board, Hitachi, Ltd.

Japan is currently in midst of a process of aging and decline of population which is proceeding in a way no other country has ever experienced. While this is often said to be the fundamental cause of the stagnation of the Japanese economy and the problem which seems to be impossible to solve, I believe that we are able to overcome this difficult situation: In fact, I consider solving this problem to be the way Japan can contribute to the world as "a forerunner in finding answers to global issues".

In this regard, I express my wholehearted respect to the Keio University's initiative to establish the Leading Graduate School Program "Science for the Development of Super Mature Society"; a comprehensive program aiming to develop talents who are able to confront the challenges of the coming decades. I have the greatest expectation for the Program's achievements.

From my perspective, what is necessary for Japan is a global leader with the flexibility to understand diversified views, and the toughness to overcome the difficulties of the tasks we face.

As a part of the development to foster such talent, it is important to provide opportunities to spend some time abroad while young. It could be an internship or a NPO activity. Such opportunities are important not only because you can improve your

2. プログラムへの期待

2.3
慶應義塾のチャレンジ、「グローバルリーダー育成」に期待して

川村　隆　株式会社日立製作所 取締役会長

　日本は今、かつて人類が経験したことがない少子高齢化と人口減少に直面しています。解決不能な日本停滞の根本原因と言われますが、私は日本がこの難題を克服しうると信じており、それこそが「課題解決先進国」として世界に貢献しうる道だと考えています。

　この時期に慶應義塾大学がリーディング大学院において「超成熟社会発展のサイエンス」をテーマに、次代を担う総合的な人材育成を開始されたことに、心から敬意を表すとともに、今後の成果に大いに期待しております。

　これからの日本に必要なのは多様性を理解する柔軟性と、直面する難題を克服するタフさを合わせ持ったグローバル人材です。

　その育成には、まず若い内に海外経験を積むことが必須です。インターンシップでも、NPO等の活動でもいい。語学力を磨くのは当然ですが、早い時期に異文化に触れ、多様性を実感することが大切だと思います。

　また、海外の経営者と付き合って気付くのは、彼らが哲学や歴史等に造詣が深いことです。いわゆるリベラル・アーツを深く学んでおり、それが発想の原点になっています。専門分野を超えた幅広い教養と高い見識を持った人材でないと、世界では通用しません。

　そして、現実の課題に向き合い、困難に挑戦し、やり遂げることで、

foreign language abilities, but also because you will be able to encounter different cultures and find out for yourselves the cultural diversity at an early stage of your life.

What I admire about my foreign counterparts whenever I meet them is their deep knowledge of, for instance, philosophy and history. They became learned in the education of liberal arts in the university days, which are at the basis of their ideas. You will not be able to succeed globally if you do not have a respectful wisdom and a profound vision.

Equipped with these qualities, tough leaders will emerge once they confront real-world issues, challenge the difficult task, and accomplish their mission.

For a country like Japan where there are no natural resources, developing talents is the only growth strategy available. It is important for business, government, and the academics to acknowledge this fact, and to cooperate with each other in developing talents that are capable of adapting to the realities of globalization.

I sincerely hope that the Leading Graduate Program, which brings together the disciplines of both social and natural sciences, will become the main source of providing such talented youth.

(2012 December)

2. プログラムへの期待

タフさを備えた真のリーダーが育ってくると考えています。資源の無い日本にとって、人材育成こそが唯一の成長戦略です。産官学が認識を共有し、力を合わせて、グローバル化に対応しうる人材育成を進めていかねばなりません。

文理融合のリーディング大学院がその輩出拠点となることを、心から願っています。

(2012年12月)

2. ANTICIPATION OF KEIO'S PROGRAM

2.4
Learn in Both Eastern and Western Ways

Guest Professor (Part-time)
Ichiro FUJISAKI
Keio University, Former Japanese Ambassador to the United States of America

Life is only once and short. In that short period one may encounter chances and risks.

Some people often say, young people should not hesitate to take risks. Be careful. Those are lucky ones who were successful. In reality, there are many more who have not succeeded than those who have succeeded. Those who failed often do not speak up.

You have to be patient to wait for the chances and to be quick to grab them. In doing so, the important thing is to recognize or identify what are the chances and what are the risks.

The decision is yours. But, references can be helpful. The best of those is learning about other people's experiences. How they made their decision. How they made their success. How they failed. Of course, in the end, these are only references. But, it can give you some hints as well. Then, how should we learn from others?

Today, American university education is deemed highly. Discussions and debates make one think. Case studies are efficient way of learning from other's experiences. But, in the long run, are university graduates so different in Japan and the United States? When I was in the government, I never felt that American or other countries officials are better negotiators than us Japanese. My

2. プログラムへの期待

2.4
日米双方のメリットを活かす

藤崎一郎 慶應義塾大学特別招聘教授、
元アメリカ合衆国駐箚特命全権大使

　人生は一度切りでしかも短い。その間にチャンスもあればリスクもある。若者は躊躇するな、リスクをとれと言う人が多い。用心したほうがいい。そんなことを言うのはきっと自分自身が幸運に恵まれ成功した人だろう。でも本当は成功した人より、しなかった人のほうがはるかに多い。失敗した人は声を挙げない。それだけのことだ。

　チャンスは忍耐強く待って、来たらパッとつかまねばならない。そのとき大事なのは何がチャンスか何がリスクか見極める力だろう。決めるのはあくまで自分自身だ。でも助けになるものもある。一番参考になるのは他人の経験だ。どうやって決断したか、成功の秘訣は何か。なぜ失敗したか。もちろん人は人だ。参考に過ぎない。でもヒントにはなるかもしれない。

　いまアメリカの大学教育が高く評価されている。たしかに議論や討論する自らの考えをまとめるのに役立つ。ケーススタディは人の経験から学ぶいい方法だ。しかし、である。教育の産物である卒業生は日米でどんな差があるか。政府にいたときアメリカであれどこの国であれ先方の代表、官僚にわれわれ日本側がかなわないなと思ったことは一度もない。理由は簡単である。日本のシステムでは会社でも役所でも十年も離れた年代の間で競争することはない。だから先輩は安心して後輩を教育し、経験を伝えていける。会社や役所が学校の代わりをしているのである。

explanation is simple. Unlike in other countries, in Japanese institutions, one is not competing with someone 10 years senior or 10 years junior. Different generations do not compete. Thus, senior members train younger generations or pass on their experiences to the latter without feeling that they may be taken over by younger ones. Companies, government institutions have thus been providing what universities have not been able to do.

The reason I was impressed with the Keio Program for Leading Graduate School is because it is exactly designed to capture good side of American education and Japanese institutions' training.

Learning from lecturers from various fields. Have private sector middle management officials as big brothers or sisters in the class and discussing ideas with them. That is the most efficient way of learning from other people's experiences.

I am certain that this program will be a model of graduate courses in many institutions in the years to come.

(2014 February)

2. プログラムへの期待

　慶應大学の博士課程教育リーディングプログラムに感心したのは、アメリカの大学教育と日本の組織内の訓練のいいところ取りをしていることである。
　いろいろな分野の講師を呼ぶ。クラスに企業の中堅幹部がいつもいて議論に加わる。まさに他の人の経験を学ぶ最も効率的な方法である。
　このプログラム、将来の高等教育のモデルになるのは間違いないだろう。

(2014年2月)

2. ANTICIPATION OF KEIO'S PROGRAM

2.5
Adaptability, Entrepreneurial Spirit and the Ability To Meet Challenges at the Interface of Multiple Domains: Here are Educational Objectives of the Keio University Program of Excellence

Professor
Arnaud POITOU
Director, Ecole Centrale de Nantes, France

As a major international university, Keio University is currently concerned with the deep and fast developments of our global society and especially education in the global context. Keio University has now launched the "Keio Leading Graduate School Program", which focuses on the major part Japan and can play in educating new world leaders. This visionary program focuses mainly on "Science for Development of Super Mature Society" and aims at counting Keio University as one of the world leading universities of the future. It is asserting the legitimacy of Keio University in contributing to the development of major strategic issues in Japanese higher education. Keio University scholars commit themselves in progress in research, providing appropriate environment including Operating and Managing Systems.

Ecole Centrale de Nantes acknowledges the importance of the project and shares Keio University's goals and concern for research & innovation development. Ecole Centrale de Nantes will be honoured to contribute to the project as a result of the historic partnership between both institutions.

The relationship between Ecole Centrale de Nantes and Keio University has been highly successful for the last twenty-five years. It currently covers scientific and cultural exchanges for

2. プログラムへの期待

2.5
適応力・起業家精神・そして多彩な分野におけるチャレンジを支援する慶應義塾大学リーディングプログラムの教育目標

アルノー ポワトー
エコール サントラル ナント校校長、教授

　慶應義塾大学は、現在、国際的な総合大学として、教育及び世界的な視点で、急速に発展を遂げ深まりつつあるグローバル化社会に関心を向けています。その一環として、慶應義塾大学博士課程教育リーディングプログラムは、日本を拠点とし、新しい世界的なリーダー教育を目指し動き始めました。この革新的なプログラムは『超成熟社会発展のサイエンス』に焦点を合わせ、将来、慶應義塾大学が世界を先導する大学として発展していくことを目的にしています。このことは、日本の高等教育を通して慶應義塾大学が戦略的課題の発展に大きく貢献することを強く示唆しています。したがって、慶應義塾大学の研究者はプログラムの管理・運営を含む適切な環境を整え、研究の発展に大きく寄与することになるでしょう。

　エコール サントラル ナント校は、慶應義塾大学博士課程教育リーディングプログラムの重要性を高く評価し、目標を分かち合い、研究や技術革新と発展に協力いたします。

　本学は、慶應義塾大学の歴史的なパートナーとしてこのプロジェクトに貢献できることを光栄に思っております。

　過去25年間、本学と慶應義塾大学は友好的な連携を行ってまいりました。現在、フランス人、日本人学生による2ヶ月から1年におよぶ学

French and Japanese students, which span from two months up to one year. More than 250 students have already benefited from our programs. Meanwhile Professors of both institutions have had regular meetings for scientific and research purposes, especially with the Faculty of Science and Technology of Keio University.

Last but not least, in March 2005, Keio University and the Group of the Ecoles Centrales signed an agreement on a Double Degree Program. Every year about 36 students contribute to the Double degree programs at Keio University and at the Ecoles Centrales.

For the last 90 years, Ecole Centrale de Nantes has aimed at training high scientific level leaders, managers and innovators fully active in the global environment. In order to achieve that goal, Ecole Centrale de Nantes has developed strong international, national and regional academic and corporate partnerships. Thanks to its international development, Ecole Centrale de Nantes now welcomes growing numbers of excellent students, researchers and academics from partner institutions in more than 50 countries. The high quality of teaching and research-engineering training programs, Master's Degrees and PhDs is fully recognized by prestigious national, European and international programs and institutions. Ecole Centrale de Nantes develops Double Degree exchange programs in the Top Industrial Mangers for Europe(T.I.M.E.) Network, including Keio University, as well as with the best universities in Brazil and China. Thanks to the Erasmus Mundus Program, Ecole Centrale de Nantes has gained a large recognition and expertise in research and international project development and management of international student mobility and partnerships.

(2013 June)

2. プログラムへの期待

術、文化的交流を行っています。すでに 250 人以上の学生がこのプログラムを利用して大きな成果を修めています。さらに、本学は慶應義塾大学、特に理工学部の教授陣と定期的に科学・研究交流も行ってまいりました。

2005 年 3 月、慶應義塾大学とエコール サントラル グループは、ダブルディグリー・プログラムの提携をいたしました。毎年、慶應義塾大学とエコール サントラル グループから約 36 人の学生がダブルディグリー・プログラムに参加しています。

過去 90 年間、エコール サントラル ナント校は、グローバル環境で活躍できる高度な科学、経営・管理、技術分野におけるリーダーの養成を目標に進んでまいりました。この目的を達成するため、強力な国際、国内、あるいは地域社会で学術機関、産業界との連携を行っています。こうした国際的な発展により、本学は現在 50 国以上に拠点を持つ連携研究機関、大学と優秀な学生、研究者、学問の交流を行っています。エコール サントラル ナント校の教育や研究者養成プログラムは、国内、ヨーロッパの権威ある国際プログラムや研究機関から高い評価を得ています。更に、本学は、慶應義塾大学やブラジル、中国隋一の大学を含む Top Industrial Managers Europe（T.I.M.E.）ネットワークとダブルディグリー・プログラムの進展をしてまいりました。また、エラスムス・ムンドゥス計画*の助成を通じて、本学は研究、国際的なプロジェクトの構築と運営、国際的な学生相互交流や連携で大きな評価を得ています。

*エラスムス・ムンドゥス（計画）：欧州の高等教育の質を高めることを目的とした、高等教育分野における教育機関の連携と、学生・学者の交流を促進するための計画です。同計画は、EU 域外諸国との協力を通じて、人と人、また異文化間の対話と相互理解を促進します。

（2013 年 6 月）

2. ANTICIPATION OF KEIO'S PROGRAM

2.6
Expectation of the Keio Program for Leading Graduate School

Professor Emeritus
Hideo AISO
Keio University, The 1st Dean,
Faculty of Environment and Information Studies

A series of discussions pertaining to the overall reform of the Keio university system began in the autumn of 1986. The goal of the reforms was to position the university to develop human resources for leadership roles in the 21st century global society. The outcome of the discussions was the opportunity to create the Shonan Fujisawa Campus (SFC) of Keio University. Three and half years of bringing together the wisdom of all school faculty members resulted in SFC's opening its doors in the spring of 1990. As an innovation motivated by society's needs, Keio's SFC was a pioneering model of university reform and has had a tremendous impact on many universities. Nearly a quarter-century has passed since SFC's opening with academia, industry, society and life having rapidly progressed and undergone kaleidoscopic changes. Consequently, the university must once again adapt to change and meet new needs.

Keio University originally proposed and has since initiated the Program for Leading Graduate School (PLGS) by focusing on "Science for Development of Super Mature Society." Unanticipated when the reform leading to SFC were developed, this new doctoral program is aimed at resolving issues that the super mature society faces. Crossing academic boundaries of faculties and

2. プログラムへの期待

2.6
慶應義塾大学
リーディングプログラムへの期待

相磯秀夫　慶應義塾大学名誉教授、初代環境情報学部学部長

　慶應義塾が21世紀の国際社会を先導する有用な人材の育成を目指して、湘南藤沢キャンパス（SFC）の創設を機に抜本的な大学改革の議論を始めたのは1986年秋のことだった。その議論は3年半にわたって、全塾教職員の衆知を結集して徹底的に行い、1990年春にSFCは開校した。SFCは慶應義塾が世に問う革新の成果であり、大学改革の先駆的なモデルとして、多くの大学に衝撃的なインパクトを与え、高い評価を得た。それからほぼ四半世紀が経つが、その間の学術・産業・社会・生活などの分野は急速に進歩し、目まぐるしい変革をもたらし、その結果として大学は改めて新しい役割が求められるようになった。

　慶應義塾大学が自ら提案し始めた高度博士人材育成活動「超成熟社会発展のサイエンス」プログラムは、正にこれから急速に進展する社会を担う人材を育成するために、大学の斬新な教育・研究のあり方を追究し、その実現案をいくつか提示したものと考えられる。この新大学院プログラムは、各研究科間の枠を超えた諸学問横断的なアプローチで成熟社会が直面する問題解決を図る高尚な思考に基づいており、理想に近い画期的なアイデアがいくつも具体化されつつあり、SFCの改革でも見られない魅力に溢れている。対象とする課題の規模はまだ小さく、試行の段階にあり、学問領域としても確立されていないが、これからの大学の新しい

departments, the program is built around a common core of achievable goals and concrete themes. These themes are anticipated to be core to society's needs in the future and academic disciplines in then own right. As the program matures, it will face challenges related to globalization of education and research. Reform of curricula and an all-round education will target social system reform for complex social issues, the development of social entrepreneurs, strengthening of collaboration among industry, academia and government and an establishment of healthy financial base. After the Ministry of Education, Culture, Sports, Science and Technology ends its support for PLGS, I have a great hope that Keio's PLGS will continue to challenge itself as the common intellectual property of all faculties and departments of Keio University.

(2014 June)

2. プログラムへの期待

教育・研究基盤にも有用な必須構想として高く評価され、今後の大学院教育・研究の中核に成長するものと確信している。本プログラムが成熟するためには、教育・研究のグローバル化・カリキュラムの整備・真のエリート教育・複雑な社会問題を解決するための社会システム技法・社会起業家の育成・産学官連携の強化・健全な財政基盤の確保など未知の課題を追究する必要がある。それだけに、本プログラムは文部科学省の研究支援が終了した後も、慶應義塾の全研究科共通の知的資産として追究し続けることを期待している。

（2014 年 6 月）

2. ANTICIPATION OF KEIO'S PROGRAM

2.7
Expectations for Leader Development in the Program for Leading Graduate School

Hirotsune SATOH

Managing Executive Officer, Head of Division,
Human Resources Division, Nippon Steel & Sumitomo
Metal Corporation. A Member of Board Council,
The Program for Leading Graduate School (All-Round)

This program, the Program for Leading Graduate School (PLGS) (All-Round), has started in 2012 to develop leaders who possess a comprehensive viewpoint, innovative planning skills, and strong management capabilities based on solid expertise. Because I see the development of human resources who can pioneer a new age to be of paramount importance for industry, I personally serve as a member of the program's board and provide what little help I can by dispatching mentors to it.

A characteristic of the program is that it fuses humanity and science; in other words, it takes an "all-round" approach. From my experience in corporate recruiting and education, I feel that today's students have a strong attachment to their own university courses, departments, and majors, and that this attachment and bias becomes stronger as they advance through their undergraduate and graduate studies. On the other hand, the industrial world is truly "an integration of humanity and science." Consequently, it demands human resources that have ceaseless curiosity for the unknown and possess the ability to work with people in other fields, whether they are in Japan or abroad. Moreover, such human resources will be essential in leading Japan—a country where a sense of stagnation keeps sometimes a rein on a path toward

2. プログラムへの期待

2.7
リーディング大学院プログラムにおけるリーダー育成へ産業界から期待する

佐藤博恒 新日鐵住金株式会社 常務執行役員
人事労政部長、博士課程教育リーディングプログラム
(オールラウンド型) ボード会議メンバー

　骨太の専門の上に、俯瞰力、独創的な企画力、高いマネージメント力を持った次世代のリーダー育成プログラムが 2012 年にスタートしました。新たな時代を切り拓く人材の育成は産業界にとっても最重要のテーマであり、私自身がボード会議メンバーとして参加するとともに、メンターも派遣して微力ながらお手伝いをさせていただいております。

　このプロジェクトの特長は「文理融合(オールラウンド)」であることです。企業で採用や育成に携わった経験から、最近の学生さんは出身の学部学科や専攻分野に対するこだわりが強く、さらには学部、修士と進むにつれてそのこだわりと思い込みが、強くなっていく傾向があるように感じます。他方、産業界はまさしく「文理融合」そのものであり、未知の世界に不断の好奇心を抱き、異なる分野の人たちと国内外を問わず連携していけるような人材を求めておりますし、閉塞感すらある日本を成長に導く為にも必須な人材です。リーディング大学院プログラムでは主専攻と副専攻だけでなく、リサーチアシスタント(RA)の多様性自体が「文理融合」を実現しており、多様なメニューと熱意あふれるスタッフの下で「文理融合」人材同士の切磋琢磨によるハードな日々が続いていると伺っております。知力・体力・気力が漲る若者のみがチャレンジできる厳しく長いプログラムですが、ランナーである RA の皆さんがゴールされた先により多く

growth. Within PLGS, research assistants (RAs) are realizing "an integration of humanity and science" not only by pursuing their first and second majors but also through their very diversity. I understand that each and every day is a determined quest for self-improvement and learning among people who seek such fusion under a broad-ranging study menu and dedicated staff. The program is a long and tough journey that only young people with vast intellectual strength, physical stamina, and mental toughness can complete. Knowing this, I, as a member of the program's board, will endeavor to enhance the advice and assistance I provide to RAs so that they will be greeted by an even broader array of possibilities and options when they reach their set goals. I very much look forward to seeing all of you step forward and achieve a great success in society.

(2014 December)

2. プログラムへの期待

の可能性(選択肢)が広がるよう、ボード会議メンバーとしてさらなる助言と支援を継続していきたいと思っております。皆さんの社会への進出とご活躍を心待ちにしております。

(2014年12月)

2. ANTICIPATION OF KEIO'S PROGRAM

2.8
Some thoughts of the Keio Program for Leading Graduate School

Norihiko FUKUDA
Mayor, City of Kawasaki

Having celebrated the 90th anniversary of its incorporation as a city last year, Kawasaki possesses outstanding potential in numerous areas. This potential can be found in Kawasaki's promotion of future-oriented industries, such as biosciences, health, welfare, the environment, and energy. It is also evident in the community development measures Kawasaki is undertaking in collaboration with diverse actors in such areas as culture, the arts, and sports.

As the mayor, I intend to utilize our city's potential to move steadily forward with municipal administration that makes full use of both wisdom and innovation. I will strive to create a "Kawasaki model" in various fields with an eye to our 100th anniversary in 10 years and to disseminate it to the entire country.

On the other hand, we—not only Kawasaki City but also Japan as a whole—face a mountain of contemporary issues involving multi-tiered factors that cannot be resolved through efforts in a single field alone. Among them are society's shift toward population decline, further manifestation of a falling birthrate and aging population, a shrinking working-age population, and deterioration of urban infrastructure.

Given that the next generation of leaders will be tasked with confronting these issues of unparalleled complexity and difficulty,

2. プログラムへの期待

2.8
慶應義塾リーディング大学院プログラムによせて

福田紀彦 川崎市長

　昨年、市制90周年を迎えた川崎市は、生命科学・健康・福祉・環境・エネルギーなど将来性のある産業の振興、また多様な主体との協働による文化・芸術やスポーツのまちづくりなど、優れた数多くのポテンシャルを持っています。

　私は、こうした川崎の多様なポテンシャルを活用して、知恵と工夫を凝らしながら市政運営を着実に進め、10年後の市制100周年に向けて、いろいろな分野で川崎モデルを作り、全国に発信していきたいと考えています。

　一方で、川崎市のみならず我が国全体にも共通する課題として、人口減少への転換、少子高齢化の更なる進展、生産年齢人口の減少、都市インフラの老朽化など、一つの分野だけでは解決できない複層的な要因を持った今日的課題が山積しています。

　こうしたこれまでに例を見ない複雑・困難な課題に立ち向かう次世代のリーダーには、スペシャリストでありながらゼネラリストとしての俯瞰力、あるいはゼネラリストでありながら特定（専門）分野に卓越した知識・能力を有する、そうした人材が求められていると思います。

　慶應義塾大学リーディング大学院プログラムでは、文理融合による革新的な教育と研究を通じた、深い専門性と幅広い総合性をともに備えた

we will need people who possess the ability to see things from a panoramic perspective as generalists while also being specialists or, alternatively, who possess superior knowledge and capability in specific fields (i.e., specialties) while remaining generalists.

In this regard, I sense that the Keio Program for Leading Graduate School is an extremely ambitious undertaking. It seeks to cultivate strong leaders who possess both thorough expertise and a broadly comprehensive viewpoint through innovative education and research that fuse the humanity and science.

To all research assistants, I ask you to step forward with self-confidence, valuing each and every encounter you have in the program.

After you complete, I look forward to seeing you create new social frameworks as you also devise and realize sustainable scenarios.

(2015 February)

2. プログラムへの期待

骨太のリーダーの育成を目指す、大変意欲的な取組であると感じています。

　RAの皆さんにおかれましては、プログラムを通じて得られたいろいろな出会いを大切にしながら、自分を信じて進んで欲しいと思います。

　そして、このプログラムを修了した暁には、新しい社会の仕組みを創り、持続可能なシナリオを描き、実現されることを期待しています。

（2015年2月）

2. ANTICIPATION OF KEIO'S PROGRAM

2.9
A Great Hope for the Keio Leading Graduate School Program: To Cultivate Graduate Students to Have Dreams and Achieve Them

Professor
Hiroshi NAGANO
National Graduate Institute For Policy Studies,
Chair of the Global Science Forum, OECD

It is said that Japan has been despondent for the last twenty years. The cause is unique: the society has failed to mobilize a variety of talented people including women and foreigners. The recent Japan is defeated in 'intelligent wars', but not in its manufacturing capability. In foreign countries, there are many Ph.D graduates within the workforce in industry and government. These valuable human resources dare to face unforeseen challenges and to seek a clue(s) for solutions. Their salary is thus quite high and their unemployment rate is low. Without integrated education of humanities and sciences, this would have not been accomplished. Universities in all over the world have been competing each other to educate such talented people.

What type of people would seek unforeseen challenges? They are people who have abundant curiosities. Is curiosity natural or innate? I believe that any curiosity stems from experiences that ones gain until the mid twenty of age. Speaking a gap term, the experience that I have gained for a year abroad during my study at the Faculty of Science and Technology in Keio University, is the one that became most valuable of my life.

Because of mobility of people, the biggest challenge that Japan is facing is to establish a society where everybody would be able

2. プログラムへの期待

2.9
夢を描き行動にうつせる人材を育む
リーディング大学院に

永野 博 政策研究大学院大学教授、
OECDグローバルサイエンスフォーラム議長

　この20年、日本は元気がないといわれています。その原因は明瞭で、女性や外国人を含め、才能ある多様な人材を活用していないことです。現在の日本は、海外諸国に対してものづくり（技術力）で負けているわけではなく、知能（知力）戦争で負けています。外国に行くと、政府でも民間企業でも、博士修了者にたくさん会います。博士は、未知の課題に立ち向かい、解を見つけようとする人たちで、給与も高いし、失業率も低い。いわゆる文理融合の柔軟な思考力なくして、そんなことはできません。世界の大学はそのような人材の養成に、大学の存亡をかけて競争しています。

　では、どんな人が未知の課題に勇敢に立ち向かえるのでしょうか。好奇心のある人です。好奇心は生まれつきのものでしょうか。私は、20歳台半ばくらいまでの体験に強く依存するのではないかと思います。最近の話題の一つにギャップタームがあります。私自身は慶應義塾の工学部に在学中、1年間休学して世界をまわったことが、その後の人生で一番役に立ち、私の人生を豊かにしてくれたと思います。

　日本の直面する最大の課題は、モビリティ（人の移動）の増加により、すべての人が能力を発揮できる社会を実現することです。これからの学生には、自らの土俵を固定せず、卒業したら、大きな夢、問題意識を持っ

to fulfill each individual's ability. I have a great hope that after graduation, graduate students will be able to take an active role in local communities or in developing countries or anywhere without fixing location but with their dream and keen awareness on local and global issues. By achieving what I am hoping for, Japan will become the most attractive place in the world. I am sincerely hoping that the Keio Leading Graduate School Program will become the place where graduate students will be cultivated to fulfill their dream and achieve beyond what I can imagine.

(2013 March)

2. プログラムへの期待

て、地方でも、途上国でも、好きなところで、好きなことで活躍してほしいと願っています。そうすれば日本自体が世界の人々を惹きつける場所となるでしょう。慶應義塾のリーディング大学院が、私には想像できない夢を描いて、実際に行動にうつせる大学院学生を養成するプロジェクトとなることを心より祈念しています。

（2013 年 3 月）

2. ANTICIPATION OF KEIO'S PROGRAM

2.10
To Demonstrate the Vitality of Japan's "Super Mature Society" at the 2020 Olympic and Paralympic Games in Tokyo to World

Professor
Mutsuko HATANO
Program Coordinator for Leading Graduate School, Tokyo Institute of Technology

After a career in research ranging from fundamental technologies to product development at a corporate laboratory (Hitachi, Ltd.), I decided to take the plunge into the unknown world of university education when I reached the age of 50. I made this decision based on my belief that "education is of paramount importance from now on." I am now focused on cultivating global leaders who will create new values and innovation with a foremost attention to students. As the director of the "Academy for Co-creative Education of Environment and Energy Science" (ACEEES), which is a participant in the Program for Leading Graduate School (PLGS), I am in a constant struggle to ensure that our 25 participating departments are striving to reach their goals. Moreover, in the area of research, I am nurturing the seeds of new creation by forming teams consisting of differing fields and institutions.

What will be needed for the development of the "super mature society"? (The truth is, when I heard that Keio University was applying for PLGS under this key phrase, I felt that we were scooped!) I believe the answers are integration, mobility, and diversity. My belief comes from what I witnessed during Silicon Valley's golden age, when inspiration was born through mutual contact among the top minds of diverse fields. Such inspiration

2. プログラムへの期待

2.10
東京オリンピック・パラリンピック 2020 で「超成熟社会」の活力を世界に披露

波多野睦子 東京工業大学教授
東京工業大学リーディングプログラムコーディネーター
（慶應義塾大学理工学部卒業）

　私は企業（日立製作所）の研究所で基礎から製品開発までの研究に従事し、半世紀の歳を迎えたとき、「これからは教育が最重要」と大学という未知の世界に飛び込んだ。学生への思いを原点に置き、新たな価値とイノベーションを創生するグローバルリーダーの育成に意を注いでいる。同じリーディング「環境エネルギー協創教育院」の院長を務め、参加 25 専攻がゴールに向かうよう悪戦苦闘している。また研究でも分野も機関も異なるチームを結成し、新たな創造の芽を育んでいる。

　「超成熟社会」（このキーワードでリーディングに応募、と伺ったときに、やられた、と感じました！）の発展には何が必要か？　融合、流動性、ダイバーシティであると信じている。これはシリコンバレーの最盛期に、異分野の精鋭が触発し合い、インスピレーションが生まれ、淘汰と生残りを通して最終的にイノベーションとなるプロセスを目の当たりにしたからである。また本人に「その気」があればチャンスは公平、多様性に対する受容力があるグローバルな社会を体験した。比して大学はディスプリンの垣根はかなり高い。そこで教育院の学生には、自分の研究分野の枠から出て、新たな課題を自ら発見し解決することにチャレンジさせている。目標があれば異分野の垣根を溶かすことができ、超領域分野でのイノベーションの創生を実感しはじめている。結果として教員へ拡がればと

ultimately grew into innovation through selection and survival. It also comes from my experience in a global society that offers fair opportunities and is receptive of diversity when people have the courage and confidence to innovate. In contrast, university disciplines have fairly high barriers. Thus, we have ACEEES students take on the challenge of stepping outside their areas of study to independently find and resolve new issues. If students have a goal, they can break down the barriers standing between fields and begin to truly experience the birth of innovation which goes beyond fields. I would like to see this also spread to teachers as a result.

With 2020 positioned as a "milestone year," I look forward to seeing PLGS graduates of Keio University, the Tokyo Institute of Technology, and other institutions succeed as central players of Japan's young generation and demonstrate to the world the vitality of our nation's increasingly diverse "super mature society."

But, what am I talking about?! This is supposed to be a forward, but the reality is... Just this morning, I again criticized my husband by saying "Stop using lots of butter like you did as a kid. Why do you still do that even after 30 years of marriage?" It seems that I can't even live my own life by respecting differences...

(2014 July)

2. プログラムへの期待

期待する。

　2020年をマイルストーンの年と位置付け、慶應、東工大をはじめとするリーディング卒業生たちが若手中核として活躍し、ダイバーシティが進む超成熟社会の活力を世界に示すことができれば、と楽しみにしている。

　ってね！？　巻頭言ですから、でも現実は。今朝も夫に、「沢山バターつける小さいころからの慣習やめてよ！　結婚して30年も経つのにどうしてよ。」と難くせつけました。違いを尊重しながら生活、なんってことはできませんわ……。

（2014年7月）

3. EXPECTATION FOR HIGH-LEVEL Ph.D. IN GLOVAL SOCIETY

3.1
The Third Opening of Japan and High-level Postgraduate Human Resource Development

Vice President
Toshiaki MAKABE
Keio University

The 20th century was opened with the quantum theory. There was an unfortunate event in which atomic bombs were used in the world war, but now, the development of microelectronics has made a society of Information Communication Technology (ICT), and produced a global society. In such a global society, information can be instantly shared in the world. Now, the geopolitical situations have been drastically changed. At present in the 21st century, our desire cannot stop at all, and the development of ICT is even accelerating toward the world of micro-photonics at the aim of creation of tools with a super-high speed and a large capacity. On the other hand, the rapid development of economy has brought various problems such as the global warming, the ozone destruction, and the depletion of fossil energy. We are now facing the great challenge of sustainability of the earth.

Such a globalization is also rapidly proceeding in Japan, and it is sometimes called as "the Third Opening of Japan" to the world. But, its construction has been quite different from the previous openings. The First Opening took place by the end of Edo Era, and the Second Opening happened after the World War II. This ongoing Third Opening has been intended to develop our super-mature society in the aging society with a low birthrate after the economy

3. 高度博士人材への期待

3.1
第三の開国と大学院高度博士人材育成

真壁利明　慶應義塾 常任理事

　20世紀は量子論とともに幕が明け、原子兵器が大戦で使用される不幸な出来事もあったが、マイクロエレクトロニクスの発展がIT社会を生んだ。その結果、情報が瞬時に共有されるグローバル社会が出現し、地球上の地政学的状況は一変した。21世紀のいま我々の欲求は留まるところを知らず、ICTは超高速で大容量なツールの開発を目指し光エレクトロニクスの世界へとその歩みを速めている。一方で、経済の急速な発展は温暖化、オゾン層破壊、化石エネルギーの枯渇など、地球の持続可能性を問う大きな課題を我々に突き付けている。

　グローバル化が急速に進むいまを第3の開国と呼ぶこともある。その構造は江戸幕府の終焉による第一次開国、世界大戦後の第二次開国と大きく異なる。経済が頂点を極めた後の少子高齢化社会のなかで、加えて3.11の東日本大震災からの復旧・復興の下で超成熟社会の発展へ向けての開国でもある。被災者の冷静で忍耐強い姿が海外で高く称賛された一方で、危機に際してリーダーの情報発信能力やコミュニケーション能力の危うさが露呈したことも記憶に新しいところだ。まさに近代史最大級の自然・人工災害という大きな打撃は、自然科学の教育と研究に携わる我々に自然に対する理解がいまだ未成熟であることを思い知らしめた。同時に、現代科学が社会インフラをリスク管理する際、社会常識と不整

has passed its peak. This should be accompanied by recovery from the Great East Japan Earthquake of March 11 in 2011. It is fresh in our memory that the victim's calm and patient attitude was highly praised internationally but at the same time questions were raised about our leaders' ability of information disclosure and their communication skills at a crisis. We have been engaging in education and research of natural science but we were shocked by such the worst natural and man-made disaster in the modern history, and learned that our understanding of the nature is still incomplete. In addition, it has been uncovered that a conflict occurs between the peoples' common sense and the modern science, when the social infrastructure is managed by the modern science. When we re-design the modern society at present, I believe it is reasonable to give a clue to solve complicated and difficult problems that often demand compromises by using the Policy Studies as well as the Pure Science cooperatively. And such a way should bring us to the Global Standard. Unfortunately, we have no existing example of an advanced nation with super-mature society; therefore, Japan has to make a solitary start domestically and internationally for a renewed civilization and further industrial development.

At all times, the society has been counting on universities a lot. Now, the high-level human resources development, which is an original mission of university, is an urgent issue and the society is eagerly expecting the universities to solve it. It is regrettable that even after 150 years of import of Western science, a chain of human powers to create science, evolve it to a technology, and pass it on to the society with great ambition, has not reached enough to a level of maturation in Japan. At present, it is necessary to act on a renovation of the framework of education and research. Our previous passive educational system with overemphasis on knowledge should be renovated to an active one that makes students learn the "ability to find a clue for solving various problems by considering, judging and making presentation for themselves".

3. 高度博士人材への期待

合な点があることも露呈した。いまあらためて都市社会の在り方を制度設計する際、学術としての科学(Pure Science)に加えて政策の科学(Policy Studies)が車の両輪の役割を演ずることで、複雑でしばしばトレードオフとなる難問の解決にその糸口を与えてゆくのが道理であり、世界標準(Global Standard)への道であろう。超成熟社会先進国として手本の無いなか、国内外に向け新しい文明とその産業発展の開拓をスタートする孤独な船出でもある。

いつの時代も社会が大学に期待するところは大きい。大学の本分、高度人材育成が待ったなしの段階を迎え、社会から熱い視線が注がれている。西洋科学を移入して150年、科学を興し、これを技術に昇華し、高い志の下で社会へ還元する一連の力が十分に成熟していないのは残念だ。この時機、教育と研究の仕組みを知識偏重の受身型から、学生が「自ら考え判断し表現することで、様々な問題を解決する糸口を見つける能力」を身につける能動型教育システムへのレノベーションが時代の要請だ。専門分野で非凡な能力を伸ばし、そのスキルを土台に、関連する経営・政策・行政などの分野で力を発揮できる底力を持った、いうなれば複雑な融合課題に接した際、その取組の鳥瞰図をしっかり描き発信するスキルを身に付けた、高度博士人材の育成と輩出が少子高齢化の下で超成熟社会の発展にとって要となろう。

慶應義塾の目指すオールラウンド型プログラムでは、地政学的な空間を意識しないキャンパス環境の下で、大学院修士・博士課程5年間のカリキュラムを構築している。プログラムに申請し競争的に採用された大学院生には、本人が所属する研究科の正指導教員に加えて、海外大学、企業や他研究科等から指導資格のある副指導教員が用意される。多様な価値観を持った医療・理工・政策・社会科学分野の教員や、産官からの豊富なキャリアを持ったメンターが集まる「水飲み場」で「超成熟社会発展のサイエンス」活動を行う。骨太の専門スキルを磨き、その分野の枠を超えてオールラウンドの立場で、社会や産業界で個を生かすための人

3. EXPECTATION FOR HIGH-LEVEL Ph.D. IN GLOVAL SOCIETY

This is a need of the times. I believe that the key for the development of the super-mature and aging society with a low birthrate is to raise and launch talented fresh PhD human resources. Such PhD people should have cultivated their special ability in their field to acquire their strong power by which they can show in various fields such as management, policy formulation and administration on the basis of their own skill. In other words, they should possess the skill for drawing and presenting the overview of efforts to be made when they face a complicated and entangled issue.

In Keio University, a five-year curriculum from the master's to doctor's course is constructed in a campus free from any constraint due to geopolitical atmosphere. For the sake of the students who have been selected for the program by competition, a team of supervisors in their department as well as qualified supportive vice-supervisors will be arranged from foreign universities, enterprises, other departments and so on. The education of the "science to strengthen the super-mature society" will be conducted in a platform called "water hole", where the professors having diverse sense of values in the research fields of medicine, science and technology, policy and social science are gathering with the mentors from industry and government. This is the place where the students should develop steady skills in a specialty and then, as all-rounders beyond their own field, they learn and polish humanity by which they show their own individuality. In addition, when people would like to extend their career by studying at foreign partnering universities, working as interns at member enterprises of the consortium, or choosing a company to work, the "water hole" will serve as a platform to make acquaintance with other people or get advice from them. The graduate students will be able to achieve more and more fruitful career and life by building up a diverse and international network of personal relationships. This is not an easy program for the participating students, but in addition to degrees of master and doctor in their major, I hope that they

3. 高度博士人材への期待

間力を鍛え学ぶ場となる。この「水飲み場」は海外連携大学への留学、コンソーシアム企業へのインターンシップや就職先選択へと、キャリアを広げる際の出会いや助言の場ともなる。グローバル化の時代、大学院生は多様で国際的な人脈に触れることで、その後のキャリアと人生を、2倍も3倍も豊富で実りあるものと出来よう。活動する学生にとって決して楽なプログラムではないが、経済的な支援の下で専門分野の修士号と博士号に加えて副専攻の修士号を取得し、そのキャリアを社会へ還元することに自覚と誇りを持ってほしい。

　グローバル化が進む現在、宇宙船地球号の上で点灯する黄信号はどれも多様な分野の専門知識を動員して、文理両面から解決の糸口を見出す類（たぐい）の大規模で複雑な課題だ。特に、日本が抱える課題は大きい。オールラウンド型リーディング大学院プログラムで巣立つ博士人材が、彼らの骨太の専門に加え、国際的な社会性と倫理性の気概を持って、企業あるいは行政分野のなかで、グローバル社会を牽引するトップリーダーとして活躍する時代の到来を私は予測している。小さくとも豊かで精神的に充実した成熟社会に移行する際、経済が右肩上がりの時代に確立された制度の見直しは当然で、大学もこの改革と決して無縁ではない。規格にはまった大量人材輩出方式に代わる、限られた数の高度博士人材育成に、大学は真正面から向き合っている。

(2014年1月)

should obtain a degree of master in their minor with financial aids, and they should be aware and proud of their responsibility of returning what they have obtained from their careers.

In conclusion, now the globalization is proceeding, warning signals on our Spaceship-Earth are big, and the complicated problems should be solved by collecting expert knowledge in various fields of both humanities and sciences. Especially, Japan has big issues at present. However, I anticipate that such time will come when the postdoctoral students, who have accomplished the all-round type Program for Leading Graduate School (PLGS), will have steady skills in their specialties and work actively and successfully as top leaders of this global society in enterprises as well as in administration. During the process of transition to a small but prosperous and matured society with people's satisfaction, the systems which were established at the time of booming economy should be certainly reformed, and the academia cannot be indifferent to such a reform. I would like to reemphasize that the universities are indeed tackling with the transition from the mass production of standardized graduates to the development of rather limited number of high-level postdoctoral human resources.

(2014 January)

3. 高度博士人材への期待

3. EXPECTATION FOR HIGH-LEVEL Ph.D. IN GLOVAL SOCIETY

3.2
The War for Talent Continues

Yumiko MURAKAMI
Director, Organisation for Economic Co-operation and Development (OECD) Tokyo Center

After almost 20 years of "lost decades", Japanese companies are finally starting to hire more people and inject new blood into their systems. The US economy is also now back to pre-recession peak levels of employment. It is encouraging to finally see two of the three largest economies in the world creating more jobs, but it is important to bear in mind that the recent world-wide recession forced companies in many countries to reduce their payroll expenditures substantially over a prolonged period of time. While the global job market has experienced a prolonged soft patch, "the war for talent" has not only taken a breather but on the contrary, it has continued to intensify the competition for the limited talent pool on a global basis. Since the recent financial crisis, there has been a renewed recognition among leaders in both the public and private sectors that success depends fundamentally on talented individuals who can lead their teams in a highly complex and interlinked global economy.

Even in Japan, where life time employment and a seniority system has been practiced for decades, some companies are starting to change their traditional hiring practices by bringing in much needed talent from the outside in order to compete against companies in other countries. I am pleased to learn that the Keio Program for

3. 高度博士人材への期待

3.2
トップ国際人材の獲得競争は続く

村上由美子 OECD（経済協力開発機構）東京センター所長

　日本経済は長いデフレ環境がようやく終焉を迎える兆しを見せはじめ、民間企業の採用も増え始めています。一方米国のほうもサブプライムをきっかけとした未曾有の世界金融危機からはや6年が過ぎ、直近の統計によると雇用がようやく金融危機前の水準に回復しました。このように雇用環境が改善するまでには、何年にもわたる就職氷河期が各国で続いていました。しかしその間も、"THE WAR FOR TALENT"と呼ばれるトップ人材獲得競争は、世界的な規模で過熱の一途をたどりました。指導的な立場に立つ人材は鋭い国際感覚を備えていなければならないということを、金融危機をきっかけに再認識した産業界は、国境を越えた経済活動に必要なスキルを持った高度なタレントを世界中から探しはじめました。

　年功序列や終身雇用が長年主流であった日本でさえ、最近は国際競争力をつけるために、従来の雇用慣行を改め、もっと柔軟に外部からトップ人材を獲得しようという企業が増えています。私はこのような時代のニーズに合致した人材を育成できるのが、慶應義塾大学のリーディングプログラムではないかと期待しています。インターネットの普及により、一瞬にして世界中に情報が拡散する今日、経済活動において国境という従来の枠組みは意味を成さなくなりました。弛みなく視野を広げ続ける好奇心、既成概念に囚われない柔軟な発想、未知の世界を恐れないチャレンジ精

3. EXPECTATION FOR HIGH-LEVEL Ph.D. IN GLOVAL SOCIETY

Leading Graduate School is designed to develop much needed young talent who can contribute to a fast changing and dynamic international society. In an era where information is disseminated exponentially in a matter of seconds all across the world, thanks to internet, and national borders no longer limit economic activities in most regions, students in the Keio Program for Leading Graduate School have tremendous opportunities to cultivate a keen sense of curiosity, the ability to think outside the box and to develop the appetite to take calculated risks and challenges. These are critical qualities one needs to succeed in today's global economy. I have high expectations for the next generational leaders from this program who will shape the future of Japan and the world.

(2014 September)

神と迅速な行動力。このような要素を持ち合わせた若者を必要としているのが今日の世界経済です。慶應義塾博士課程教育リーディングプログラムを通じて、さまざまな分野から刺激を受け、真の国際人としてリーダーシップを培っていただくことを望んでいます。

(2014年9月)

3. EXPECTATION FOR HIGH-LEVEL Ph.D. IN GLOVAL SOCIETY

3.3
Innovative Doctoral Training

Professor
Kurt DEKETELAERE
Secretary-General of the League of European Research Universities and Professor of Law at the University of Leuven, Belgium

I am writing this piece while I am heading to the University of Oxford, to open the 6th Doctoral Summer School of the League of European Research Universities (LERU, www.leru.org). This year's topic is "Sharing Excellence-The Value of Knowledge Exchange". Previous editions focused on: "Research Integrity", "Leadership", "Open Science", "Entrepreneurship", "Communication". These themes illustrate how much importance LERU attaches to "Innovative Doctoral Training" (IDT).In the IDT-approach, the modern doctorate is (i) at its core determined by an interplay between professional research experience and personal development, the most important outcome of which is an individual trained to have a unique set of high level skills; and (ii) an excellent training for those who go into roles beyond research and education, in the public, charitable and private sectors, where deep rigorous analysis is needed. Doctoral programmes at LERU universities aim to train researchers to the highest skill levels to become creative, critical and autonomous intellectual risk takers.

Just six weeks ago, at the end of May 2015, I had the pleasure to visit Keio University and give a Career Path Lecture in the 'Science for Development of Super Mature Society Program" (Keio Program for Leading Graduate School). This program is a perfect

3. 高度博士人材への期待

3.3
想像力に富んだ博士の養成

クルト デケテレール ヨーロッパ研究大学リーグ
(LERU) 事務局長、ルーヴェン大学 (ベルギー) 法学部教授

　私は、ヨーロッパ研究大学リーグ (The League of European Research Universities : LERU, www.leru.org) 第6回博士課程夏期講座の会場であるオックスフォード大学へ向かう途中でこの記事を書いています。これまで、この講座では「研究の公正性」、「リーダーシップ」、「開かれた科学」、「アントレプレナーシップ」、「コミュニケーション」を取り上げており、今年は「エクセレンスの共有－知識交換の価値」をテーマとして開催する予定です。テーマをご覧になっておわかりのように、LERUは「革新的博士課程教育」(Innovative Doctoral Training: IDT) に重きをおいてきました。現代の博士教育は (i) 専門的な研究の経験と個人としての成長の相互作用によって本質的に決まるもので、その最も重要な成果は個々に高度なスキルを身につけた人財そのものであり、(ii) 行政や公益組織、産業界の様に深く緻密な分析力が必要とされる研究や教育の垣根を超えた様々な分野で活動する人財のための素晴らしいトレーニングの場である、というのがIDTの立場です。この立場から、LERU加盟大学の博士教育は、研究者に最高レベルのスキルを習得させ、創造的、批判的、自律的に知的なリスクを取れる人材を育てることを目指しています。

　私は2015年5月末に慶應義塾大学を訪れ、「超成熟社会発展のサイエンス」(博士課程教育リーディングプログラム) でキャリアパス講演を行

Japanese illustration of the IDT-approach. The program correctly starts from the fact that the Japanese society has tremendously changed, and a new type of doctoral students is, therefore, needed. Doctoral students who do not only possess great academic expertise, but also have a broad perspective and vision, and planning and management abilities which will be critically needed. These newly trained individuals will play a major role in the decision-making process in industries, international organizations and central and local governments. By seeking to revolutionise education and research within an integrated framework of arts and sciences, and cooperating with industry and government, the All-Round Program for Leading Graduate School (PLGS) will clearly cultivate highly qualified doctoral students and contribute to needs in the Japanese society.In talking with the PhD students which were selected since the start of the program, it became clear to me how successful the program is already now: bright people, with broad perspectives, using their academic expertise to tackle societal problems in a multidisciplinary approach, and showing the way for the further and future development of the Japanese society. Impressive and a job very well done by Keio University!

(2015 October)

う機会に恵まれました。このプログラムは、日本社会の大きな変化に伴って新しいタイプの博士課程の学生が必要になったという認識から出発しており、日本で実践されているIDTアプローチを具現化した好例です。それはまことに当を得ているといえるでしょう。博士課程で学ぶ学生は、深い学問的知識だけではなく、今後決定的に重要となる広い視野とビジョン、企画力とマネジメント力を身につけなければなりません。こうした新しい教育を受けた人材は、これから産業界、国際組織、政府、地方自治体での意思決定プロセスにおいて中心的役割を果たしていくはずです。文理を融合した枠組みの中で産業界・行政体との連携によって教育と研究を根本的に変化させようとする慶應義塾大学博士課程教育リーディングプログラム［オールラウンド型］（PLGS）は、高い資質を持つ博士を育成し、必ずや日本社会のニーズに大きく貢献することでしょう。私はこのプログラムの開始時に選抜された博士課程の学生たちと話をしてみて、この試みがすでに大きな成功を収めていると確信しました。彼らはみな聡明で、広い視野を持ち、学際的なアプローチで社会の問題に取り組むために学術的な専門知識を駆使し、日本社会の未来を切り拓く方法を世に問おうとしていました。私はこの学生たちに深い感銘を受けました。慶應義塾大学はまちがいなくすばらしい博士課程教育を実践しています！

(2015年10月)

3.4
Japan's Economy on Track by Creating New Markets with Innovation and Converting the Industrial Structure
Yoshihiko NAGASATO

Ph.D. Counselor, Asahi Research Center Co., Ltd.
Japan Business Federation, Chairman of the Sub-Committee on Industry-Academia-Government Cooperation, Committee on Industrial Technology

For several years following the collapse of the Berlin Wall, Japan's economy ranked number one in the world in terms of competiveness (IMD World Competitiveness Ranking). However, with the end of the Cold War, cheap labor markets suddenly appeared in Eastern Europe, Russia, China, Southeast Asia, South America, and other regions. The appearance of these markets marked the beginning of the so-called "lost two decades" in Japan's economy.

One of the primary factors that promotes economic growth is workforce transition. During Japan's post-war period of rapid economic growth, a major portion of the workforce moved from primary-sector industries with low productivity (in terms of per capita added value) to high-productivity secondary-sector industries. At the same time, the nation's high population growth rate provided an abundant and high-quality labor supply.

Conversely, during the "lost two decades," the workforce moved from industries with high productivity to those with low productivity. The wave of globalization and strong yen led to the downsizing of Japan's manufacturing industries and the overseas relocation of factories. Consequently, Japan's workforce moved from manufacturing and construction to new sources of

3. 高度博士人材への期待

3.4
イノベーションにより新市場を創生し、産業構造を転換して日本経済を成長軌道にのせよう

永里善彦　旭リサーチセンター相談役、
日本経済団体連合会 産業技術委員会 産学官連携推進部会長

　ベルリンの壁が崩壊したころ、日本経済は、競争力1位を数年続けていた(IMD国際競争力ランキング)。しかし冷戦時代が終わり、東欧・ロシア・中国・東南アジア・南米等の安い労働力市場が突如登場した。かくして失われた日本経済の20年が始まった。

　経済成長を促す要因の一つに、労働人口の推移がある。戦後の高度成長期には、生産性(一人当たり付加価値額)の低い第1次産業から生産性の高い第2次産業への大量の労働人口移動があり、また高い人口増加率による質の高い豊富な労働力の供給があった。

　しかし「失われた20年」では、生産性の高い分野から低い分野に労働人口が移動した。押し寄せるグローバル化の波と円高のため、製造業はスリム化し、海外に工場を移転した。その結果、日本の労働人口は、製造業・建設業から、新たな雇用の受け皿としての福祉・介護事業へと移動したが、金融保険業を除いて第3次産業は生産性が低い。そして金融業は日本の得意分野ではなかった。

　少子高齢化時代の超成熟社会では、労働人口の増大は期待できない。したがってデフレから脱却し経済成長を促すためには生産性の高い事業を創生し、付加価値の高い新しいモノづくり業を起こす必要がある。例えばサービスを見据えたモノづくり、システムを組み込んだモノづくり、

employment; namely, welfare and nursing care businesses. However, with the exception of finance and insurance, tertiary-sector industries have low productivity. And financial business was not an area in which Japan excelled.

Within our "super mature society" that is a consequence of Japan's low birthrate and aging population, we cannot expect to have a growing workforce. Accordingly, the nation must create highly productive businesses and develop new forms of high value-added manufacturing in order to break out from its current deflationary cycle and spur economic growth. Examples here include manufacturing that is focused on services, manufacturing that incorporates systems, the fusion of manufacturing with information and communication technologies, the creation of solution systems businesses, and the development of so-called "sixth-order industries" (i.e., those that combine primary-, secondary-, and tertiary-sector industries) to stimulate local economies. In other words, Japan must put its economy on track by creating new markets through innovation and converting its industrial structure. A growing economy will lead to greater tax revenue and stronger fiscal health.

The other day, when I gave a lecture on career paths, I had the opportunity to see and participate in mentors' seminar, a group project exercise (GPE). I was truly impressed by the active discussions that took place as participants attempted to find solutions to specific themes. What struck me was the way these discussions shed light on possibilities for the emergence of new high added-value manufacturing and solution systems business.

A person in the business community once said that students are "homestay students from the future." I expect that students who have completed the Program for Leading Graduate School (All-Round), which is a scheme that looks to the future, will soon apply themselves in industrial, academic, and government sectors and spread their wings on the international stage.

(2015 May)

3. 高度博士人材への期待

モノづくりとICTの融合、ソリューション・システムビジネスの創出、地域経済活性化のための6次産業の創生等々。換言すればイノベーションにより新市場を創生し、産業構造を転換して日本経済を成長軌道にのせる。経済が成長すれば税収が増えて財政健全化が図れる。

過日、キャリアパス講演を行った際に、GPE（グループプロジェクト演習）メンターゼミを見学し参加する機会を得た。具体的なテーマをもとに、ソリューションを模索する活発なやり取りに心から感銘を受けた。そこから付加価値の高い新しいモノづくり、ソリューション・システムビジネス等が生まれる可能性を見出したからである。

学生は「未来からの留学生」とある財界人が言ったが、この時代を先取りしたオールラウンド型リーデイング大学院プログラムを修了した学生が、近い将来、産・学・官の分野で切磋琢磨し、世界に羽ばたく人材として活躍することを期待したい。

(2015年5月)

3. EXPECTATION FOR HIGH-LEVEL Ph.D. IN GLOVAL SOCIETY

3.5
Leaders with Integrated Expertise in Both Natural and Social Sciences in Developing Super Mature Society

Professor
Yoshio HIGUCHI

Dean, Faculty of Business and Commerce &
Graduate School of Business and Commerce

As the expression "the lost two decades" reflects, the Japanese economy is currently in midst of a long-term stagnation. The level of nominal GDP in 2011 is what it was 20 years ago in 1991. It implies that the economy has not grown at all during the period. Moreover, in recent years, real growth rate has fallen significantly, and nominal GDP is even showing a declining trend.

There are views emphasizing that the long-term stagnation is a result of accidental factors; inadequate responses to the recurrent disasters such as the global financial crisis and the earthquake. On the other hand, there are strong supports for the views that emphasize structural factors as the main reason; the Japanese economy, which is facing decline in number of children and aging of the population as well as further globalization of the economy, has lost competitiveness and is witnessing hollowing-out of the industry as a result of its inability to raise productivity and the lack of introduction of new products that stimulate demand.

In the past, Japanese firms were the front-runners of the global economy, leading the firms of other countries. In contrast, the same firms are facing a big wall standing in its way and seems as though they have lost sight of the way to go: the Japanese economy is suffering so much. While enjoying the wealth that had been

3.5
超成熟社会発展に求められる文理融合リーダー

樋口美雄　商学部長・商学研究科委員長・教授

　日本経済は、「失われた20年」と表現されるように、長期にわたって低迷を続けている。2011年の名目国内総生産は20年前の1991年と同水準にあり、経済はこの間、まったく成長しなかったことになる。ましてやここ数年来の実質成長率は大きく低下し、名目GDPは縮小傾向さえ示している。

　日本経済が長期にわたり停滞を続けているのは、相次いで国際的金融危機や震災に見舞われたためであり、これに適切な対応ができなかったためであるという偶発的要因によるという見方をする人がいる。その一方、人口の少子高齢化が進展し、経済がグローバル化する中、日本経済は生産性を向上させることができないまま、需要を喚起する新製品も登場しなくなった結果、競争力を失って、空洞化しつつあると、構造的要因を主因に挙げる見方も強い。

　かつて日本企業は世界経済の先頭に立って、各国企業を牽引してきた。それが今、大きな壁が企業に立ちはだかる一方、新興国の急激な追い上げにあって、進むべき方向を見失ったのではないかと思われるほど日本経済は苦しんでいる。過去の成功により蓄積された豊かさを人々は享受する一方、将来に向けては重い空気が漂っている。

　こうした「超成熟社会」のフロンティアを切り開き、その壁を打ち破る

accumulated by the successes in the past, there is a sense of opacity toward the future.

As means to break through the barrier and extend the frontier of "the Super Mature Society," a lot is expected from technological innovation. New technology not only increases firms' competitiveness, but also vitalizes economic activity and greatly changes the lives of the people. I probably wouldn't need to refer to the example of the invention of steam engines in the 18th century England to persuade you that technological innovation sometimes plays the role of priming for creating a new civilization.

It goes without saying that advancement of science and engineering, and medicine is essential for the creation of new technology. However, to create new technology on a sustained basis, the role of political and social sciences is also important. Even though one often says that "necessity is the mother of invention," it does not mean that if there is a necessity, new invention will inevitably be created.

For the industrial revolution to take place in England, appropriate environment had to be prepared. England, in those days, had many colonies that provided raw and intermediate products while, at the same time, needed new products. The Puritan and the Glorious Revolutions prepared social and economic environment for expanding markets, and capital accumulation for easier fund-raising. Furthermore, agricultural revolution prepared the basis for providing labor force. It is because these conditions were met that utilization of coal was able to replace consumption of charcoal that had destroyed forests till then. The use of coal, in turn, led to the invention of the steam engines that significantly improved thermal efficiency, and the successive invention of new technologies. Markets expanded and led the world into a new civilization.

Even though huge amount of money and significant number of human resources are mobilized, it does not necessarily lead to creation of new technologies that meet the needs of the society. To

ための突破口として、技術革新に対する期待は極めて大きい。新技術の登場は企業の競争力を高めると同時に、経済を活性化させ、人々の生活を一変させる。ときには新たな文明を創り出すための起爆剤になることは、18世紀イギリスの産業革命における蒸気機関の発明の例を持ち出すまでもない。

新技術の誕生に理工学や医科学の発展が不可欠であることはいうまでもない。だが、それを引き金に社会が待ち望む新技術を連鎖的に創出していく上では、政策・社会科学の果たす役割も大きい。「必要は発明の母である」といわれるが、「必要」さえあれば、社会が求める発明が必然的に生まれてくるわけではない。

イギリスで産業革命が始まったのも、それなりの環境が用意されていたからであるといわれる。当時のイギリスは、原材料の供給地であり、新製品を必要とする植民地を多数持っていた。また清教徒革命・名誉革命により、市場を拡大するための社会的・経済的環境が用意され、さらには資金調達を容易にするための資本蓄積が用意され、なおかつ農業革命によって労働力の基盤が整えられていた。こうした条件が整えられていたからこそ、それまでの森林破壊をもたらした燃料である木炭の消費に代わって、石炭の活用を可能にし、熱効率を飛躍的に向上させる蒸気機関が発明され、これが起爆剤となって連鎖的に新技術を生みだし、市場を拡大し、世界を新しい文明社会へと導いた。

研究開発に多額の資金と豊富な人材が投入されたからといって、社会の求める新技術は必ずしも創り出されるわけではない。こうしたリソースを効率よく新技術の開発に繋げていくには、それに適した法律や税制、会計制度などの社会インフラ、そして組織運営や業績評価、報酬制度などの企業プラットホームが求められる。人文・社会科学の発展は、これらの環境整備に寄与する。

たとえば知的財産権に関する保護ルールの整備である。特許法が知的財産権の保護により、企業の研究開発は促進される半面、取引に制限を

combine these resources efficiently to develop new technologies, adequate social infrastructure, such as law, taxation, and accounting system, as well as appropriate corporate platform, such as organizational management, performance evaluation, and remuneration system, are required. Developments of humanities and social sciences contribute in preparing such necessary environment.

An example of this aspect is the establishment of protection rules with regards intellectual property rights. While patents stimulate firms' R&Ds by protecting property rights, there is a possibility that diffusion of knowledge and development of industries are hindered by restricting trade. According to a research John McMillan, Reinventing the Bazaar: A Natural History of the Markets, W.W. Norton and Co. Inc., contracts with non-competition duty is acknowledged by the law in Massachusetts, U.S. so that workers are prohibited, for some period of time, to use what he has learned from the former employer for the benefit of the new employer. It protects the fruits of the firms' R&Ds but diffusion of the new technology to the region and collective development are hindered: It is said that the development of the Route 128, which used to be a center of IT industry, came to a halt as a consequence.

In contrast, such contracts were not acknowledged in California so that workers of competitive firms established open relationships with one another, and through engineers' frequent change of jobs, so it is explained, the development of Silicon Valley was achieved. However, it does not necessarily means that weak protection of intellectual property rights always contribute to regional technological progress. Whether it succeeds or not depends on such factors as the amount of investment the firm has to make initially, and the speed of innovation.

How to incorporate non-financial information, such as intellectual property rights and human assets, to the accounting system; how should taxation and academic evaluation systems,

設けることで知識の普及や産業の発展を妨げる可能性がある。ある研究（ジョン・マクミラン著『市場を創る』NTT 出版）によると、米国マサチューセッツ州では、競業避止契約が法的に認められており、社員が前の企業で学んだことを転職先で使用することは一定期間禁止されている。これにより企業の研究開発の成果は保護される一方、地域への新技術の普及や共同開発は阻止され、かつて IT 産業の中心地であったルート 128 地区の発展にブレーキがかかったという。

これに対し、カリフォルニア州ではこの規定が法律により認められていなかったために、競合企業の社員同士がオープンな関係を築き、エンジニアの頻繁な転職を通じ、シリコンバレーの発展がもたらされたことが示されている。だが、常に弱い知的財産権保護が地域の技術進歩に貢献するとは限らない。その成否は企業が必要とする初期投資額の大きさやイノベーションの速度によって異なる。

知的財産や人的資産などの非財務情報をどのように会計制度に組み込んだらよいか、そして税制や研究者の評価制度、報酬体系、情報共有や協業、そして研究者倫理はいかにあったらよいか。研究開発の成果にこうした社会インフラは大きな影響を与える。これらの研究成果に与える効果を統計に基づき実証分析し、研究基盤整備に活かすことも社会科学の一つの役割である。

「超成熟社会」において、新たな豊かさをもたらす上で、技術革新の果たす役割は極めて大きい。研究開発が成果を上げ、超成熟社会の次のフェーズを切り開いていくには、産官学連携の下、理工学、医科学、政策・社会科学が文理融合した知見を兼ね備えたリーダーの登場が求められる。

（2013 年 1 月）

remuneration system, information-sharing and collaboration, and ethics of researchers be; the way such social infrastructure develop have significant influence on the outcome of R&Ds. Making statistical analyses of the impact of such infrastructure on outcomes of researches, and making most of their results in establishing the foundations for research is also the role that social science should play.

In "the Super Mature Society", the role that technological innovation has to play in bringing about new wealth is significantly important. In order to increase the fruits of R&Ds, and open-up the next phase of the super mature society, wanted are the leaders with expertise integrating science and engineering, medicine, political and social sciences, fostered by a joint effort of the industry, the government, and the academia.

(2013 January)

3. 高度博士人材への期待

3. EXPECTATION FOR HIGH-LEVEL Ph.D. IN GLOVAL SOCIETY

3.6
Expectations for Leaders

Atsushi MIURA
Deputy Mayor, City of Kawasaki

As unprecedented it is in the world, Japan will become a super-aged society with a decrease in the population. In contrast, the city of Kawasaki has been increasing its population, particularly that of younger generations, presently reaching to 1,440,000 in total. Nevertheless, low birth rate and longevity is about to become our own reality in the city as well. In fact, it is predicted that the population of the city might start decreasing in Heisei 42 (in 2030). As exemplified by long-lasting public facilities and compact city in our mid and long term perspective and life innovations, green innovations and welfare innovations in a part of our own growth strategies, we have been working on creating a self-sustainable city in the face of the present challenge.

In order to accelerate these our efforts, the city of Kawasaki and Keio University have singed a basic agreement on an exchange of human resources and development of scientific technologies in Heisei 21 (in 2009) and have established a variety of research developments as a collaborate effort of industry, academia and government on K2 town campus near Shin-Kawasaki. In particular, we have our high expectation for Keio Program for Leading Graduate School, since our city needs to foster professional people with an excellent expertise as well as broadly trained knowledge.

3. 高度博士人材への期待

3.6
川崎市が期待するリーダー像

三浦　淳　川崎市副市長

　日本は世界に類を見ない超高齢・人口減少社会を迎えようとしています。そうした中、人口144万人を擁する川崎市は、現在も若い世代の流入を背景に人口増加が続いていますが、少子高齢化は着実に進行しており、平成42年（2030年）には人口減少を迎えることが見込まれています。本市ではこのような状況を踏まえ、公共施設の「長寿命化」「コンパクト化」など中長期的な視点によるまちづくりや「ライフイノベーション」「グリーンイノベーション」「ウェルフェアイノベーション」など川崎の強みを活かした成長戦略により持続可能なまちづくりを推進しています。

　この取組を加速するため、慶應義塾大学とは平成21年に人材交流の推進や科学技術の振興などで連携・協力するため基本協定を締結し、新川崎に立地するK2タウンキャンパスにおいて産学官連携による研究開発を推進するなど、様々な取組を進めています。特に、博士課程リーディング大学院プログラムに対しては、本市としても高度な専門性に加えて総合性を有する人材の育成が求められていることから、大きな期待を寄せています。

　現在、本市からメンターを派遣して学生に対する指導・助言を行っていますが、学生の研究内容を見ると本市の課題認識と共通する部分もあり、本プログラムは今後の超成熟社会において想定される課題の解決に向け

Our city has been sending a mentor to the leading program and we have shared our outstanding issues with some research projects of research assistants (RAs) in the program. Therefore, we are confident that the program will play an essential role in solving potential issues in the super mature society.

To offer a challenge to RAs, our city have been giving them omnibus lectures on city policy including urban planning and welfare, since RAs are required to seek real issues in the super mature society and carry out their research. We are, thereby, hoping that this leading program will be able to cultivate doctoral students as the future leaders.

(2013 October)

3. 高度博士人材への期待

て大変意義深いものであると感じています。

　本市としては、学生自らが超成熟社会の抱える現実的な課題をしっかりと捉え、研究活動が行えるように、まちづくりや福祉など様々な分野から課題提起を行うオムニバス講座を提供してまいります。本プログラムにより世界をリードし、次世代を担う博士人材が輩出されることを心から願っています。

(2013年10月)

3.7
Development of Global Mindest, Skill and Leadership

Professor
Tojiro AOYAMA
Dean, Faculty of Science and Technology & Graduate School of Science and Technology

The Program for Leading Graduate School (All-Round) (PLGS) as Science for Development of Super Mature Society was launched at Keio University two years ago. To date, graduate students, as research assistants (RAs) enrolled in 2012 and 2013, have been working on their course work and participating in various activities of the program. For the future of our country and a construction of prosperous future societies of industrialized nations, this leading program is presently thriving to cultivate leaders who will be charged to seek resolution of a variety of outstanding issues under the backdrop of emerging our super mature society we have never encountered before.

In the five-year leading program offering master through doctoral graduate degree programs, PLGS have provided the unique double-degree master program by integrating arts and sciences and aiming at cultivating leaders with overall abilities and skills. The program fosters RAs to approach outstanding issues of their own expertise with a fruitful knowledge of engineering, political and social sciences and/or medical sciences. In several years, the first graduates of RAs will embark on their journey in a society. One of the most important attributes for their future contribution will be their global mindset and human skill and strength.

3. 高度博士人材への期待

3.7
豊かな国際力の育成

青山藤詞郎 プログラム委員、
理工学部長・理工学研究科委員長・教授

　慶應義塾大学博士課程教育リーディングプログラム「超成熟社会発展のサイエンス」がスタートしてから、2年目の秋学期を迎え、第1期、2期生は大きな志を胸に、日々勉学に励んでいます。人類の歴史において経験したことがないと言われている超成熟社会の到来を目前にした我が国の将来と、同様な問題を抱えている先進諸国の人々の豊かな未来社会構築の為、諸問題の解決を託すことができるリーダーの育成を目指して本プログラムが稼働しています。

　5年間にわたる修士から博士学位取得までの一貫教育プログラムでは、修士課程における文理融合型ダブルディグリープログラムとしてのユニークな教育プログラムを提供し、自らの主専門領域に付して工学的、政策・社会学的あるいは医学的側面に関する豊かな知識と経験を身につけた、総合力豊かなリーダーの育成を目指しています。数年後には、最初の修了生が慶應義塾から世に羽ばたくことになりますが、彼らが将来にわたって活躍するための重要な資質の一つとして、豊かな国際力とこれを支える人間力が挙げられましょう。

　本リーディングプログラムは、今年度よりフランスのエコール サントラル ドゥ ナントの積極的な協力を得ることなり、プログラムの国際性がより強化されることになりました。同校のアルヌー・ポワトゥ学長に心より

PLGS has also started a wonderful collaboration with Ecole Centrale de Nantes (ECN), France, this year, an active participation of the ECN that strengthens the program further internationally. We express our sincere gratitude to the President, Professor Arnaud Poitou, of ECN. Since ECN and Keio University have had an international partnership for more than 25 years, I am strongly confident that this long and fruitful collaboration will become a driving force for further development of PLGS.

For the super mature society to achieve sustainable development of social and industrial transformations, it would be not merely Japanese but global challenges to solve these daunting problems. We will need to cultivate global leaders who possess their mindset beyond a boundary of nations and understanding of social structures in different cultures and play an active role in a global society.

(2013 December)

感謝の意を表します。同校と慶應義塾大学は、25年間以上にわたり友好的な連携の歴史があり、この豊かな経験をベースとした協力関係は、本プログラムの推進に大きな力となるものと確信しています。

　超成熟社会を迎え、これを支えるための社会構造と産業構造の転換は、決して日本国内だけで解決される問題では無いことは言うまでもありません。国の垣根を越えて、異なる文化に基づく種々の社会構造を理解し、世界で活躍できるグローバルリーダーの育成が強く望まれます。

（2013年11月）

3. EXPECTATION FOR HIGH-LEVEL Ph.D. IN GLOVAL SOCIETY

3.8
To The Keio Program for Leading Graduate School

Takemitsu KUNIO
Senior Vice President, NEC Corporation

On 7 December, I had an opportunity to give a lecture at the Keio Program for Leading Graduate School (PLGS). Entitled 'My Career Path – A Creation of A New Value', I lectured graduate students on the current status and issues of the Information and Communication Technology industry that have dramatically grown after the World War II and discussed the change in values that the products and services have provided to customers over the years.

In the lecture, I have summarized two periods of the status and issues of the Information and Communication Technology industry. Up to the early period of 2000, the driving force for industry growth has been the continuous development and advancement of scientific technologies including the transformation of electronic circuits to semiconductors, digitization of information, miniaturization of sensor elements, and from a customer point of view, the value for 'a shorter processing time and miniaturization of the system' was embraced by many. On the other hand, after 2000, the most valuable factor for products was shifted to the ease of use and represents the importance to integrate human and medical aspects with the traditional science and technology aspects of value.

In the discussion session of my lecture, a number of students

3. 高度博士人材への期待

3.8
生産性高い議論の場から育つ博士人材に期待して

國尾武光　日本電気株式会社　執行役員

　去る12月7日、リーディングプログラムにて講義をする機会を得た。講義の題目を「私のキャリアパス〜新たな価値観の創出〜」として、戦後飛躍的な成長を遂げてきた情報通信・情報処理産業の現状と課題を学生諸氏に説明し、「製品・サービスが顧客に与える価値」の時代的変化を論じた。

　講義の主旨は我が国の情報通信・情報処理産業において、2000年初頭までの成長を支えてきたドライビングフォースが、電子回路の半導体化、情報のデジタル化、センサー素子の小型化等、まさに科学技術の進展・深化であり、顧客視点で述べれば、「処理時間の短縮・システムの小型化」という価値観が多くの顧客に受け入れられてきたこと、一方、2000年以降、「人にとっての使い易さ」が製品の価値を決める重要な因子と変わり、単なる「理工学」的価値観に「人文科学・医学」的価値観を複合化することの重要性が増してきたこと、を概説することにあった。

　講義後半に設定した討議時間では、多くの学生が率直に自分の考えを述べるとともに、本質的な質問を当方に投げかけてくれた。これらの質疑を通して私が感じたことは、物怖じしない態度、学生同士のインターラクティブな討議の多さであった。いろいろな大学でしばしば講義を行うが、今回ほど質疑が充実したことはなかった。これらのことを分析すると、

have expressed their own opinions and addressed fundamental issues to me. The session has provided me with a strong impression that, with very interactive discussions among them, the students were not scared but open-mined. Among the lectures that I have given in different universities, the discussion in this lecture was thus most extensive and productive. Each question and discussion led to a series of subsequent questions and discussions, consequently deepening the whole session. In other words, it was a testimony that, by listening carefully to others' opinions, understanding all with their own thoughts and then combining their own questions and opinions, the session has created the most extensive and productive discussions among all participants.

As the Keio PLGS has a theme, to solve issues on 'Development of Super Mature Society', it is inevitable to coordinate and integrate a number of academic disciplines. The coordination and integration of different disciplines requires an attitude and flexibility that one needs to listen carefully to others' opinions, to make an effort to coordinate and integrate one's own opinion with others and to accept others' opinions. The students I have met and shared opinions and discussions with all possess their quality to satisfy this requirement. Therefore, I have spent a great moment with them in the lecture.

(2014 May)

一人の質疑が他者の質疑を呼び起こし、議論の幅・厚みが拡がったことにあると感じている。これらは人の話をよく聞き、自分なりにそれを咀嚼して、今度は自分の疑問・意見を重ねていくという、本当に生産性の高い議論ができたことにあると思う。

　本大学院のテーマである「超成熟社会を発展させていく」という課題の解決には、複数の学問を複合的に連携させていく必要がある。学問の複合化には、他者の意見を傾聴し、自らの意見を重ねていく努力と複合化された意見を受け入れる柔軟性が肝要である。その資質を十分に感ずることができる学生諸氏と時間を共有できたことは、私にとって有意義な出来事であった。

（2014年5月）

3. EXPECTATION FOR HIGH-LEVEL Ph.D. IN GLOVAL SOCIETY

3.9
Never Give Up

Ryo KUBOTA
MD, PhD. Founder, Chairman and CEO, ACUCELA Inc.

I have changed my career every 10 years: I started as a researcher, then I was an ophthalmologist and then in 2002, upon founding Acucela, I became an entrepreneur. And this year, 2014, I began my journey as a public company CEO when Acucela became the first US company to list on the Tokyo Stock Exchange.

I have been able to pursue such a vast and creatively-driven career because I embrace risk and have realized the power of never giving up. I believe that if you work hard on something and dedicate yourself to a goal, the process, whether it ends in success or failure, will help you build important skills and you will come to know and understand great lessons. If you continue the process of trial and error, your success rate can go up and you can reach your goal faster. Once I realized "I can change myself if I keep striving," I became a person who is action oriented and who has avoided becoming "stuck" in non-action. I have often taken the route less travelled and found that there is value in trying to do something that hasn't been done before.

If you keep challenging yourself and working hard, you will be successful. Of course, sometimes things don't go as planned or you may notice that this is not what you want for the rest of your life. You may also notice that it is not as interesting as you were

3. 高度博士人材への期待

3.9
あきらめないこと

窪田　良　アキュセラ インク　創業者、会長兼 CEO

　私は 10 年ごとにキャリアチェンジをしてきました。研究者として 10 年、眼科医として 10 年、起業家として 10 年、そして今年、上場企業の経営者としての挑戦が始まりました。私がこういうキャリアを歩めたのは、楽観的だから潔く次に進めたのもありますが、小学校の頃に「諦めない力」に目覚めたからだと思います。失敗を含め、何かに真剣に取り組んだプロセスそのものが自分の力を高めてくれる。価値ある失敗を繰り返せば、着実に成功確率はあがり、より早く目標に到達できる。「地道に努力を続ければ自分は変われる」ことがわかってからは、迷うよりも実行するタイプの人間になりました。リスクを恐れず前例がないことこそ我が道だと考えるので、あえて人とは逆の道を選ぶこともしばしば。

　挑戦をし続ける、努力をし続ける先には成果が必ずあります。うまくいかないこともあれば、人生をかけて追究したいほどではないと分かる結果が待っていることもある。ものすごく興味があったとしてもいざやってみるとそれほどでもないことはあるものです。例えば迷っている興味の対象が 100 個あるとして、そこから 1 つ減れば 99 個になり、段々と最もやりたいものに近づくわけです。その最後の 1 つにたどり着く過程で自分の知識や専門性は深まり、直感も研ぎすまされます。やり続けることに無駄はありません。生涯をかけて実現したい夢が具現化する道が見えてき

originally thinking. If you have 100 things that you are interested in and you try one of them, you then have 99 things that you can try and you will gradually reach to what you want. By the time when you try the last one, you will improve your knowledge and expertise with a keen instinct. Nothing will be a waste by trying. You will see what you want to do for the rest of your life. What you want to do becomes very clear and you will know your goal. The goal is a key to choose your career. You never know what the outcome will be unless you try. So if you are wondering, please just try first and never give up.

(2014 November)

3. 高度博士人材への期待

ます。内在的にぼんやりしていたものが1つのしっかりした目標になる。その夢こそがみなさんのキャリアパスの軸になるのではないでしょうか。

　どんな成果が待ち受けているかはやってみないとわからないので、「どうしよう」と思うならまずはやってみてください、そして諦めないで続けて下さい。

（2014年11月）

3.10
Expectation for High-level Ph.Ds.

Kaoru KUZUME
Corporate Auditor, Marubeni Corporation. A Member of Board Council, The Program for Leading Graduate School (All-Round)

As its birthrate falls and its society ages at an unprecedented pace, Japan is experiencing a decline in its national power vis-à-vis other countries that is in parallel with its shrinking population. At the same time, Japan's overseas influence continues to wane. If Japan is to maintain and enhance its presence amid these trends, particularly given the expected arrival of a "super mature society" in the 21st century, it must cultivate first-rate individuals who simultaneously possess an international perspective and creativity founded on deep thought and broad knowledge.

Launched with the goal of developing international leaders, the Program for Leading Graduate School (PLGS) has entered its fourth year. Its first group of graduates will begin to make their way in society in 2017.

To the research assistants (RAs) in the program, I say this: I hope to see all of you make a good start by striving to become role models, not only for those who will be coming through the program behind you, but also for boys and girls who also dream of one day becoming leaders in the world's various fields. Of course, regardless of how talented you are, you will leave the program as young people who have yet to experience the real world. Nationally-led industry-academia-government will provide essential

3. 高度博士人材への期待

3.10
リーディング学生への期待

葛目　薫　丸紅株式会社 監査役、PLGS ボード会議メンバー

　史上例を見ない急速な少子高齢化の下、世界の中での日本の国力は人口減と並行して縮小しており、海外での発言力も小さくなりつつあります。21世紀の来るべき「超成熟社会」に於いて、少子高齢化した日本がそのプレゼンスを維持・向上させて行くには、国際的な視野と深い思考・広い学識に基づく独創力を兼ね備えた優れた個の育成が不可欠となります。

　世界を牽引するリーダー人財の育成を目指してスタートした当プログラムも4年目を迎え、再来年には第一期生を社会に輩出します。

　RAの皆さんには、後に続く後輩のみならず、将来、世界の様々な分野で、リーダーとしての活躍を夢見る少年少女たちの憧れの存在になるべく、良いスタートを切って頂きたい。勿論、いくら優秀であっても、プログラムの出口では、皆さんは未だ社会経験のない若者であり、国を挙げた産学官のバックアップは必要不可欠ですが、その前に、一人ひとりが自ら課題を見つけ、目標に向け取り組んで行く「セルフ・スターター」タイプの人間となり、自分自身の更なる価値向上のため、不断の努力を続けて頂かなくてはなりません。当プログラムは、目的でもゴールでもなく、あくまでも世界のリーダーへのスタートであることを改めてご認識頂くことが重要です。

support for you. However, even before this, each one of you must make unceasing efforts to further enhance your own value and become a "self-starter" who autonomously finds challenges and achieves goals. It is important for you to remember that this program is neither an objective nor a goal. It is merely the start of your path toward international leadership.

Speaking personally, I believe the largest hurdle facing today's Japanese is "an extreme lack of young people who can confidently look people from other countries in the eye and who can debate issues and make their points in a non-combative manner." What is important here is the ability to understand the viewpoints of people from other cultures and to discuss issues with them with his or her own spirit. This takes not only language ability but also the skills and scholarship needed to maintain one's position in the face of opposition as well as a firm grasp of one's identity as a citizen of Japan. I believe that those people who possess these qualities are the ones capable of becoming "global human resources."

When it comes to such "skills and scholarship," all of you are continuing to acquire a broad range of expertise and language ability through the program. I urge you to use the fruits as a foundation for considering for yourselves what you must now do to become an international leader and for taking steady and ambitious steps toward becoming a true asset for the world. I have great expectations for you all.

(2015 July)

3. 高度博士人材への期待

　個人的意見として、現代の日本人の最大の課題は「外国人の目を堂々と見つめて、喧嘩することなく議論し、論破できる若者が極端に少ない」ことだと思います。言語力のみならず、これだけは誰にも負けないというスキルと学識、そして日本人としてのアイデンティティをしっかり持ち、ぶれることなく異文化の相手の話を理解し、議論を進めることが重要であり、それが出来る人こそグローバル人財となり得るのではないでしょうか？

　皆さんは、「スキルと学識」については、既に当プログラムで幅広い専門知識・語学を修得しつつあります。今後は、それをベースに、世界のリーダーとなるために自らが今為すべきことは何か、自ら考え、高い志を持って着実に取り組み、真のグローバル人財の魁となって頂きたいと思います。大いに期待しています。

（2015 年 7 月）

3. EXPECTATION FOR HIGH-LEVEL Ph.D. IN GLOVAL SOCIETY

3.11
Leadership Aptitude: Is it Inherent or Acquired ?

Professor
Fumihiko KANNARI
Program Coordinator

Some three years since its start, the education program (Program for Leading Graduate School, All-Round) and its operation are approaching a state of normalcy. My expectations are growing for the first-term students who have grown strongly together with the program, and I am seeing elements of development of human resources from new perspectives as students' specialties become more diverse with each passing year. Creating leaders who can succeed on the global stage within the five-year period of this program is, of course, impossible. Nonetheless, I believe we can test the program's success by looking at the degree to which it nurtures the qualities needed to become a leader.

Finding what various prominent figures think with regard to the question of "what is leadership" is not hard. However, I believe a leader must be able to quickly grasp circumstances, pertinent information, and surrounding viewpoints as they pertain to a given problem; to make timely decisions based on firm values; to issue decisions with courage and readiness to take responsibility; and to always remain consistent. What is important is the ability to gather information and analyze others' viewpoints until a decision can be made and then to predict how the information and viewpoints will change going forward and ultimately make a decision, even if that

3. 高度博士人材への期待

3.11
先天的か後天的か：リーダーの資質

神成文彦　プログラムコーディネーター、理工学研究科教授

　プログラムスタートから約3年をかけ、教育プログラムとその運営はほぼ定常状態に近い形になり、プログラムの構築と共に逞しく育ってきた1期生への期待が膨らむとともに、毎年加わる学生の専門分野が多様になるにしたがって、新たな視点での人材育成の要素に気づきを得ている。本プログラムを5年で修了した出口において、グローバルに活躍できるリーダーを作り上げることは所詮不可能であるが、リーダーに必要な資質をどこまで芽生えさせることができるかが本プログラムの試金石となる。

　「リーダーとは」という問いに対して多くの著名人の考えを見つけることができるが、私は、リーダーに求められるのは、与えられた課題に対して、短時間のうちに状況、情報、そして周囲の意見分布を把握し、確固たる価値観の上にタイムリーに判断を行い、責任所在の覚悟の上に勇気をもって決断を下す、そして決してぶれないことにあると考える。重要なのは、決断するまでの情報収集と他人の意見の分析、その上でのこれからの展開を予測し、リスクも敢えてとることも含めて判断できる能力である。それらの混沌とした要素の渦の中であっても、自分がよりどころとする価値観をしっかりと築けている人間は、決断を下すことができる。その価値観の源は、判断を求められている専門性における学問の深さ、加えて歴史、哲学、時事等の広い教養であり、そしてこれまでの経験である。

decision may even be risky. One who has firmly cultivated values that he or she can depend on, even when the above elements are chaotic, has the ability to make decisions. These values come from the depth of the person's scholarship in his or her area of expertise where a decision is required, as well as a broad background in history, philosophy, current affairs, and other educational fields. And then, of course, there is the one's own past experience.

Recently, personnel officers in industrial circles have been using the phrase "shuraba taiken" (experience in hell). This phrase describes precisely the kind of training that is needed to cultivate values. In other words, it is possible to give a person values through the development of acquired skills. However, there is a viewpoint that a leader possesses abilities that he or she was born with. Among people who have succeeded in business ventures, there are those who publicly state that their success was largely due to aptitudes they were born with. However, I would like to believe that, just as people can use only a portion of their brain cells, success comes from how people cultivate the aptitudes all of us are born with, and this is where education and experience-based learning can play a role in. I do not believe we can simply speak of students who are enlightened by their self-awareness and dare to boldly participate in a difficult program of human resource development in terms of differences in aptitude alone.

(2015 January)

3. 高度博士人材への期待

　最近は、産業界の人事担当者から修羅場体験という言葉を聞くが、まさにそのための訓練をさすのであろう。これらは、後天的な能力開発で授けることが可能である。しかし、そもそも、リーダーとは生まれながらに持った才能ではないかという側面もある。ベンチャーマインドも、生まれながらの資質の要素は大きいと公言するベンチャー成功者もいる。しかし、人間は脳細胞の一部しか使いこなせないように、誰もが生まれながらに有する資質をいかに芽生えさせるかであり、それは教育、経験学習が担うことができるものと私は信じたい。自己の気づきに啓発され、敢えて困難な人材育成プログラムに果敢に参加している学生諸君を素質の差で片づけるわけにはいかない。

（2015年1月）

Chapter 2
Program for Leading Graduate School (PLGS): Framework and Current Status

Introduction

Program Coordinator
Fumihiko Kannari
Professor, Graduate School of Science and Technology

The economy and social system of many advanced nations have developed, providing abundant resources and services for a free and convenient lifestyle. At the same time, as growth peaks and values among individuals diversify, we are faced with a society with multiple issues. In Japan, the problem of rapidly declining birth rates and an aging population compounds the situation, further complicating these issues. The focus is now shifting from quantity-based satisfaction to a better quality of life (QOL), causing a major transformation of values, or a paradigm shift, in society. This societal reformation is by no means limited to negative implications. We can instead interpret it as a new social system that applies the latest technology or as an opportunity to rethink the state of education and community and generate new forms of convenience and accessibility. In a society that is dynamically changing on a global scale, could our graduate education system produce talented individuals who are capable of becoming new forms of leaders in the industrial sector, international organizations, and platforms of national and regional policy-making, while yielding broad perspectives, unique planning abilities, and superior management skills as well as solid expertise? The objective of this project is to build an educational program for this purpose,

第2章
リーディング大学院プログラム
―その仕組みと取り組み状況―

はじめに

プログラムコーディネーター
神成文彦　理工学研究科教授

　多くの先進国は、経済や社会制度が発展し、必要な物やサービスは満たされ、自由で便利な生活はできるが、成長がピークに達し、それにともなう価値観が人々の間で多様化し、色々な状況を呈している社会を迎えています。日本は、さらに急速な少子高齢化の問題がこれに加わり、さらに問題が複雑化しています。これまでの、量的満足度から、生活の質（QOL）を高めることに焦点が移っており、価値観の大きな変化（パラダイムシフト）が社会に起きています。ただし、この社会の変革においては、決して負の要因だけではなく、最新の技術を応用した新しい社会システム、教育やコミュニティーのあり方についての再考、新たな利便性などを生み出すだすチャンスと位置付けることもできます。こうした、地球規模で大きく変化する社会において、産業界、国際機関、国・地方の政策決定の場で、骨太の専門の上に、俯瞰力、独創的な企画力、高いマネージメント力を持った新しい型のリーダとなりうる人材を大学院教育から輩出できるか、そのために必要な教育プログラムを現行の学問教育システムとの整合性をとりつつ構築していくことが、本プログラムのミッションです。

　本プログラムにおいて、リーダーとしての素養としてとくに重点を置くのがグローバル性です。ただし「国際性」と言われていた旧来型の国際経

while coordinating with the academic system that is currently being implemented.

In this program, we are placing particular emphasis on nurturing global leaders. However, this is not limited to traditional expectations for "internationalism," such as overseas experiences and conversational skills. The skills that truly global human resources must develop include the abilities to analyze themselves and others, analyze the culture of their own country and those of others, respect the diversity of values while swiftly recognizing commonalities, present their own perspective and explain it to groups of various backgrounds, make fair decisions, and take action. These skills can actually be gained without international experience and instead cultivated through processes such as collaborating with those in the arts and sciences, collaborating with those of differing interests, and uniting academia and industry. The goal of this program is to foster human resources that could not be developed with only dedicated focus on expertise or international experiences limited to the field of expertise, as seen in doctoral education in the past.

Three years after the program began, the education program and its administration has reached a largely steady state and are gaining insights about the cultivation of human resources from a new perspective. It is, in fact, impossible to fully develop globally active leaders by the end of their five years in this program, but our touchstone is the extent to which the program could nurture necessary leadership qualities. There are opinions among many prominent figures regarding "what it means to be a leader," but I believe that leaders are required to quickly grasp the situation, information, and opinions of those around them when faced with a given problem; form timely judgments based on firm values; make the decision with courage and resolution to take responsibility; and never waver. The important thing is to have the ability to make judgments, including gathering information and analyzing the

験、会話能力だけを指すのではなく、真のグローバル人材には、自己・自国文化分析力と他者・他国文化分析力、価値観の多様性の尊厳と共通項の素早い見極め、自らの考え方の開示とバックグラウンドの異なる集団に対する説明能力、公平な判断・行動力などの能力開発が必要となります。これらは、国際経験の中だけからしか育成できないわけではなく、むしろ文系・理系の人間や異なる利害関係をもつ者との共同作業、アカデミアと産業の融合作業、などからも教育できる能力であると考えます。従来の博士課程教育における、専門性のみの追究、あるいは専門分野を通してのみの国際経験では育むことのできなかった人材育成が本プログラムの目的です。

プログラムスタートから約3年をかけ、教育プログラムとその運営はほぼ定常状態に近い形になり、新たな視点での人材育成の要素に気づきを得ています。本プログラムを5年で修了した出口において、グローバルに活躍できるリーダーを作り上げることは所詮不可能ですが、リーダーに必要な資質をどこまで芽生えさせることができるかが本プログラムの試金石となります。「リーダーとは」という問いに対して多くの著名人の考えを見つけることができますが、私は、リーダーに求められるのは、与えられた課題に対して、短時間のうちに状況、情報、そして周囲の意見分布を把握し、確固たる価値観の上にタイムリーに判断を行い、責任所在の覚悟の上に勇気をもって決断を下す、そして決してぶれないことにあると考えます。重要なのは、決断するまでの情報収集と他人の意見の分析、その上でのこれからの展開を予測し、リスクも敢えてとることも含めて判断できる能力です。それらの混沌とした要素の渦の中であっても、自分がよりどころとする価値観をしっかりと築けている人間は、決断を下すことができると思います。その価値観の源は、判断を求められている専門性における学問の深さ、加えて歴史、哲学、時事等の広い教養であり、そしてこれまでの経験です。

opinion of others, before making the decision and the capacity to predict the next developments and deliberately take risks. Those who have been able to construct concrete, reliable values, even within this whirlpool of chaos, are the ones who are able to make decisions. The source of these values would be the depth of learning in their field of expertise—a broad education in areas such as history, philosophy, and current events, as well as past experiences.

1. Goal and Program

Although a highly industrialized society was established in Japan during the 20th century, the "mature" Japanese society is rapidly evolving to one that is "super mature" in the 21st century—the first of its kind among advanced nations. Japan is facing issues that include (1) a lower birthrate and increased longevity and (2) an ever-lasting low-growth economy. Global warming, energy shortages, food crises, natural disasters, and subsequent recoveries challenge the sustainability of modern societies. These complex and interrelated problems more often than not require trade-offs rather than easy clear-cut choices. The daunting problems facing us are no longer solvable with the skills obtained in a single specialized academic field; it will take a new era to seek solutions by combining efforts from a number of academic fields and importantly from both arts and sciences.

In this year, leaders to be cultivated will have the following character traits: projecting a clear view and vision of how to achieve sustainable development in the face of the challenges of a super mature society; acting globally to proactively and emphatically accomplish all these challenges; being broadly trained (all-round) and possessing deep academic expertise; and being capable of establishing a new framework of society.

1. プログラムの目的

20世紀は高度産業化社会の発展の時代でしたが、21世紀に入り一転して、1) 急速な少子高齢化の進展、2) 低成長経済の定着等という、いわば超成熟社会に日本は先進国の中で最初に直面しています。そこでは、人類の持続可能性を問う地球温暖化やエネルギー・食糧問題等、複雑でしばしばトレードオフの選択を要する難問が多数出現しており、一つの専門分野ではどうにもならず、複数の文理専門分野を融合して解決の糸口を見出してゆく時代になりました。

そのような時代に、社会が求める人材とは、新しい社会の仕組みを創り、新しい産業を発展させ、国際社会を先導しながら超成熟社会の持続的な発展のシナリオを描き、それを断固として実行できる専門性と周辺総合力をともに備えた次代のリーダーです。

どうすればこのような将来のリーダーを育成できるのでしょうか。

これまでの大学院博士課程では、学術的貢献に価値をおく教育研究活動が中心でした。よってその出口は、大学教員や研究者が中心でした。今後は、このような出口に加えて、産業界で新しいマーケットを開拓する場や、国際機関や国・地方の政策策定の場で、独創的な企画力と高いマネージメント力を備えた高度博士人材がイノベーションを牽引することが

Then how should we nurture these future leaders?

It had been the norm for the value of doctoral education to be judged by its academic contributions. Therefore, the exit was leading primarily to university faculty and researchers. In addition to this exit method, however, our society will now need highly qualified doctoral students who possess creative planning and management abilities to lead innovation in the industrial sector to pioneer new markets and in international organizations or platforms of national and regional policy-making. The goal of our All-Round Program for Leading Graduate Schools (PLGS) is, therefore, to cultivate highly qualified doctoral students who can lead a sustainable development of the super mature society by seeking to revolutionize education and research within an integrated framework of arts and sciences and collaborations with industries and the government.

2. Program Outline

The goal of our All-Round PLGS is to cultivate a generation of highly qualified doctoral students by seeking to revolutionize education and research within an integrated framework of arts and sciences and collaborations with industries and the government. Five pillars will feature in our program.

2.1 Research assistantship with a stipend

In our program, nearly 20 graduate students are admitted each year on a competitive basis from 13 graduate school programs of Keio University. To make the most of this five-year program, first-year master's degree graduate students are most desirable to be enrolled. As they are appointed as Research Assistants (RAs) and are supported with a stipend, graduate students enrolled in the program must take courses and participate in various activities of the

期待されます。ここに、骨太の主専攻を基盤に、本格的な文理融合と産業界・行政体との密な連携による革新的な教育環境の中で、来るべき超成熟社会の持続的発展をリードできる次代の高度博士人材の育成・輩出を目指す本プログラムの具体的で大きな意義があります。

2. プログラムの特長

本プログラムは、骨太の主専攻を基盤に、本格的な文理融合と産業界・行政体との密な連携による革新的な教育環境の中で、次代の高度博士人材の育成・輩出を目指します。その特長は下記の5つの柱に集約されます。

2.1 RAとして修士の段階から雇用

本プログラムは、毎年度20名程度以内、慶應義塾大学大学院の13研究科在籍の学生から、本人からの申請を基に選抜します。採用された学生は、本人が所属する主専攻の研究科での履修に加え、本プログラムのリサーチアシスタント（RA）として雇用され、本プログラムが定めた共通科目やメニューに取組むこととなります。月給は、14.5～24万円／月を修士・博士課程の間に支給します（最大5年間；毎年度、評価・査定

core curriculum of the leading program, along with those in their own graduate program. RAs can mark this employment as a professional employment in their career.

The stipend ranges from 145,000 to 240,000 yen per month during the master's program through to the Ph.D. programs for up to five years, and the RAs are evaluated and assessed each year for a renewal of their stipend. This method of promotional stipend increase based on assessment creates incentives for RAs as they work toward the evaluation at the end of the year.

2.2 Implementation of an integrated education of arts and sciences

To develop broad views and visions under their major expertise, all enrolled RAs are required to follow the core curriculum in the five-year program and obtain a master's degree (the first major master's degree) (M), followed by another master's degree (the second major master degree), (M) and finally a Ph.D. (the first major doctoral degree) (D). The second major master's degree should be in a different field from the first major master's degree; the two fields together will foster RAs to greatly broaden their academic knowledge. The "joint-degree program" (See 3.1) has been newly institutionalized for the leading program in 2012. Therefore, RAs are able to obtain two master's degrees within three to three and a half years. For example, an RA with a first major master's program in the Graduate School of Science and Technology and who is enrolled in his/her second major master's program in the Graduate School of Economics or the Graduate School of Business and Commerce would be able to receive an integrated education of the arts and sciences. All experiences gained from two master's degrees will be expected to play an important role in developing broad views and visions and planning abilities upon their return to their first major doctoral program. We also realized that while RAs gain the benefits of integrated arts and

する)。査定に基づく昇給方式にすることで、年度末の評価に向けて RA にインセンティブが働きます。

2.2 本格的な文理融合環境で履修

　本格的な文理融合環境とは、大学院修士・博士の 5 年一貫のカリキュラムの中で、文系と理系のように互いに大きく異なった分野の修士号を 2 つ取得することで、学問の幅を大きく広げることです。そのため本学は、本プログラムを履修する学生向けに「ジョイントディグリー制度 (3.1) 参照)」を制定し、3 〜 3.5 年の期間に 2 つの修士号の取得を可能としました。例えば、主専攻が理工学の学生は、副専攻として例えば経済学や商学等を履修することで、文理融合を実現します。その経験が、主専攻博士課程に戻って研究を深め・展開する際に、俯瞰力や独創的な企画力となって発揮されることが期待されます。こうして RA は自らが分離融合の恩恵を受けますが、それだけではありません。副専攻で学んだゼミに参加する周辺の学生に対しても、全く違った方法論による課題解決を提案することで、新たな刺激を与えることがわかってきました。これは当初予想しなかった効果です。

sciences, other students who participate in the seminars of their second major may also gain new inspiration from the completely different methodologies used by the RAs to solve problems. This is an unexpected effect that we had not initially predicted.

2.3 The mentorship from industries and the government

Every Saturday, RAs participate in an extensive session with 11 mentors from renowned industries and a local government body. These mentors, mostly a manager (or equivalent) or higher-ranked official in their industries and/or local government body, provide RAs with real issues involved in industries and our society. The RAs are divided into small groups by mentor and discuss their issue(s), delve deeper into discussions for a necessary solution(s), and make a recommendation(s) for the government and/or industry (that is, a group project exercise). Thus, such group project exercises will be key for RAs to develop their views and visions of industries and governments, real issues in our society, and communication skills with people from renowned industries and/or local government bodies.

2.4 Internship and study abroad

Our program will offer RAs two-step international experiences: internship and study abroad. During the master's programs, RAs participate in an internship abroad, working at an industry or NPO for four weeks. During their doctoral program, for instance, RAs study abroad and deepen their major expertise for half a year in an international research institution or a university as part of their collaborative research. By staying overseas for a certain period and conducting collaborative work, they will be able to establish global connections. The leading program supports their expenses for a training of the job interview, a VISA application, round-trip airfares, and room and board.

2.3 日本を代表する企業等のメンターによる指導

　日本を代表する企業や行政体等の部長クラス11人が、RAに対する指導者（メンター）となって毎週土曜日に来塾し、産業界や社会の生の課題をRAに提供します。メンター毎に少人数にグループ分けされたRAは、メンターの指導の下で課題を掘り下げ、解決策を求めて議論を深めます。その結果は、政策／企業戦略提言に繋げます（グループプロジェクト演習）。RAは、産業界や行政体の考え方や、社会の生の課題を知るだけでなく、多様な業界の社会人との円滑なコミュニケーションの方法を学ぶこともできます。

2.4 海外インターンシップ・短期留学

　本プログラムは海外インターンシップと短期留学の2段階の海外派遣を用意しています。第1は、修士課程において、4週間程度、海外の企業やNPO等に一人で出かけて就労体験します。第2は、博士課程において、自分の専門を究めるため、例えば海外研究機関や大学と共同研究を行うために半年程度海外に滞在する短期留学です。このように海外に一定期間滞在し、共同作業を行なう中で、グローバルな人脈形成が期待できます。そのため、RA採用初年度には、少人数制の英語コミュニケーションスキル習得の機会を年間を通して設けているほか、派遣先企業との受入れ面接の訓練やVISA取得のサポートを行っています。

2.5 The waterhole effect

RAs in the program possess a variety of backgrounds since they have been selected from 13 graduate schools of different disciplines. As of the end of the 2014 fiscal year, RAs have actually been selected from 12 Graduate Schools of Letters, Economics, Law, Human Relations, Business and Commerce, Medicine, Science and Technology, Media and Governance, Health Management, Pharmaceutical Sciences, Business Administration, and Media Design. RAs are able to gain their awareness and receive stimulation in an environment where they can experience real issues provided by their mentors from a variety of industries and government bodies and discuss themes for sustainable development of a super mature society. As observed in waterholes in savannas where genetic exchanges have taken place during evolution of animals, RAs, faculty members with a diverse range of values and knowledge from 13 graduate schools, experts from a variety of industries and government bodies, and foreign scholars with a variety of experience and values all gather in the Hiyoshi Campus West Annex. In addition, these individuals will gather in summer and winter camps to present and discuss many issues together. This learning stimulation for RAs will be called the waterhole effect. Results will be presented, i.e., as a poster, in classrooms of the Hiyoshi Campus West Annex, summer and winter camps, and symposia.

3. Educational System
 —MMD System realizes genuine integration of arts and sciences—

The educational system of our All-Round PLGS will cultivate a generation of highly qualified doctoral students by combining their major expertise of selected RAs with (1) double majors for integrated

2.5 「水飲み場」効果

　RAは、13研究科から応募された学生を対象に選抜するので、RAのバックグラウンドは多様（文学、経済学、法学、社会学、商学、医学、理工学、政策・メディア、健康マネジメント、薬学、経営管理、メディアデザインの12研究科からの採用実績あり）です。多様な業種の産業界・行政体から派遣されたメンターや、本プログラムに参加する7研究科から選出された教員の専門分野や経験もまた、実に多様です。生命の進化の過程において、サバンナの水飲み場で遺伝子交配が起きたように、こうした多種多様な人々が、本プログラムの拠点に毎週集い、夏・冬キャンプでは泊まり込んで討論する場を設けており、RAが大いに触発され、多くの気付きを得ることができます。これを「水飲み場効果」と称していますが、本プログラムの活動拠点である日吉西別館や夏・冬のキャンプ、シンポジウムでのポスター発表等で実現されます。

3.　教育システム（MMDシステムによる本格的な文理融合の実現）

　本プログラムの教育システムは、採用されたRAの骨太の主専攻の上に、1) ダブルメジャーによる本格的な文理融合と、2) 産業界・行政体

education of arts and sciences and (2) an innovative education featuring collaborative efforts of academia, industries, and government.

Each year, 10 to 20 RAs are selected from first-year master's students (second-year in certain cases) who belong to any of the 13 research graduate schools at this university. This corresponds to around 1% of the first-year master's degree across the graduate schools. As of October 2015, there are 43 RAs in this program, and the distribution of the graduate schools according to their majors is below. The Graduate School of Science and Technology holds the majority, but they are also the majority in terms of the population of first-year master's students at our university; therefore, we can interpret this as a distribution that is proportionate to the graduate school as a whole. In addition, we can see that students have been gathered from diverse graduate schools, such as the Graduate School of   Letters, Economics, Law, and Business and Commerce.

In addition to fulfilling all requirements for their the first and second major master's and doctoral degrees according to the MMD educational system, RAs are required to take the core curriculum of the leading program and to participate in various activities including summer and winter camps and internships abroad. Consequently, RAs will be expected to possess broad views and visions and abilities to discover and solve complex issues, to make a plan(s) and to execute all. To complete our PLGS, RAs need to fulfill requirements for the following: 1) completion of all requirements for one of the existing graduate programs that each RA belongs to and 2) a completion of all requirements for the leading program as described above. Upon the completion of their doctoral program, the completion of the leading program will be described in a diploma. In addition, the RAs will be expected to move on to areas where they can cultivate new markets in industries or to avenues such as international organizations or platforms of national and regional policy-making.

との密な連携による革新的な教育環境を構築し、その中で次代の高度博士人材を育成・輩出するものです。

　RAは、本学大学院13研究科の何れかに属する修士1年生（一部2年生のケースあり）の中から、毎年10～20名の規模で選抜されます。それは全研究科の修士1年生の約1%に相当します。2015年8月時点で本プログラムにRAは43名在籍し、その主専攻の研究科の分布は以下のとおりです。理工学研究科が過半数を占めますが、本学大学院の修士1年生全体の母数の上でも過半数を占めているので、大学院全体に比例した分布であると見ることができます。他は、文学、経済学、法学、商学等多様な研究科から学生が集まっていることがわかります。

　RAは、MMD教育システムに沿って、本学大学院の既存の研究科の修士〜博士まで修めることに加えて、本プログラムが定めた共通科目の履修、および夏・冬キャンプや海外インターンシップ等のメニュー・イベントへ参加することで、俯瞰力や課題発見・解決能力、企画力、実行力を身に付けることが期待されます。よって、本プログラムの修了要件は、1）在籍する既存の研究科の学則等による必要な要件を満たすとともに、2）本プログラムが定めた上記履修等要件を満たすことの双方が必要です。これらの要件を満たして修了すると、博士号の学位記に、本プログラムを修了したことが附記されます。修了後は、これまでの博士とは異なった領域として、産業界における新しいマーケットの開拓の場、国際機関や国・地方の行政体における政策策定の場等に輩出されることが期待されます。

　以下、本プログラムの5年一貫の教育システムを、1）ジョイントディグリー制度を中核としたMMDシステム、2）共通科目の履修、3）夏・冬キャンプ等への参加、4）主専攻との協調、5）e-ラーニングクラウドシステムの活用の5つの項目に集約して説明します。

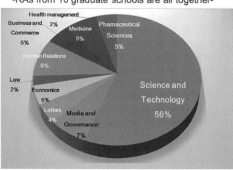

First major of 43 RAs selected in FY2012-2015
-RAs from 10 graduate schools are all together-

The educational system of our five-year PLGS is described as follows: 1) MMD system (joint-degree program); 2) the core curriculum; 3) activities including summer and winter camps; 4) a coordinated effort for each RA's first major research; and 5) use of e-Learning Cloud System.

3.1 The MMD system under an agreement of the joint-degree program (the first major master's degree, the second major master's degree, and the first major doctoral degree)

A key program of our PLGS is the MMD system where all RAs will be enrolled in the first major and second major master's degree programs and then the first major doctoral degree program. To enable RAs to finish the five-year program of the MMD system, the joint-degree program has been institutionalized as an agreement with Keio University for our leading program, allowing RAs to finish two master's degrees in three to three and a half years.

This system was established for the master's students in this program and is designed to allow students to effectively earn the credits necessary for completing the second major master's degree

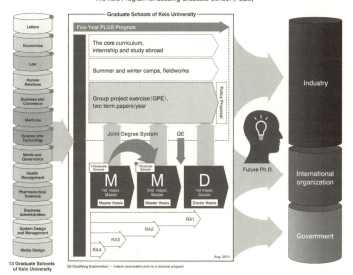

3.1 ジョイントディグリー制度を中心としたMMD(主専攻修士、副専攻修士、主専攻博士)システム

本プログラムは、骨太の専門の基盤の上に、広い視野と俯瞰力を形成するため、主専攻修士Mの後に副専攻修士Mを履修させ、その後に主専攻博士Dを履修させるMMDシステムに特徴があります。このMMDシステムを5年で修了可能とするため、本学は、本プログラムを履修する学生向けの「ジョイントディグリー制度」を制定し、3〜3.5年の期間に2つの修士号の取得を可能としました。

本制度は、本プログラムで学ぶ修士課程の学生を対象に設けられたもので、単位の先取りや読み替えにより、副専攻修士修了に必要な単位を短期間で効果的に取得可能な設計となっています。また、副専攻修士入学時の試験は、一般入試とは別枠として面接型となるほか、副専攻研究

by taking the credits in advance and replacement. In addition, the entrance exam for the second major master's program will be in an interview format separate from the general exams, with the benefit of exemption from entrance fee.

The M of the second major is chosen among 7 of the 13 graduate schools on the left side of the figure with the ● mark on the upper right, related to research in the first major as well as the arts and sciences.

3.2 The core curriculum unique to PLGS

The heart of the core curriculum in the leading program is a course of group project exercise. This course will continue through the entire five-year program. A group of RAs will be mentored by top-class experts from renowned Japanese industries and a local government body. In addition, RAs will participate in internships abroad (each for about four weeks) during master's degree programs and research study abroad (about a half year) during the first major doctoral degree program. These activities will foster RAs to broaden their internationalism and perspectives and obtain their innovative planning ability, along with their major expertise.

3.3 Various activities (including summer and winter camps)

Summer and winter camps will provide RAs with a meeting place where faculty members with different fields and mentors from a variety of industries and a local government body will gather. Participants will stay overnight under the same roof and take part in diverse activities, such as presenting the results of group project exercises and forming teams to compete for solutions of upcoming trade-off challenges. RAs will be able to sharpen their abilities by participating in active exchanges and discussions among participants with various backgrounds and a wealth of experience.

科への入学金が免除される特典もあります。

　副専攻のMは、図の左端の13研究科の内、右上に●印の付いた7研究科の一つであって、主専攻の研究と文理の関係にあるものが選択されます。

3.2 本プログラムが設置した専用の共通科目の履修

　共通科目（後述）のうち、「グループプロジェクト演習（GPE演習）」は本プログラムの最も重要な科目であり、採用から修了までの5年間に亘って履修する唯一の科目です。日本を代表する企業や行政体の部長クラスの有識者が、毎週土曜日に拠点に参集し、グループワークにより学生を指導します。

　また、学外特別研修では、修士課程における海外インターンシップ派遣（4週間程度、異文化の中で就労体験）と、博士課程における短期留学（半年程度、主専攻の研究について副指導を受ける）を課すことで、グローバル力の他、骨太の主専攻の上に俯瞰力や独創的な企画力を身に付けることが期待されます。

3.3 夏・冬キャンプ等イベントへの参加

　夏・冬キャンプは、多様な分野の教員および、多様な業種の企業や行政体から派遣されたメンターに、RAが長時間接する最も良い機会です。RAは、グループプロジェクト演習の成果を発表したり、今後のトレードオフ課題について、チームを結成してそのソリューションを競い合う等、多様な活動を寝食を共にして行います。RAは、多様な分野から集まった人生の先輩から多様な意見を聞き、じっくり討論して、自分を成長させる良い機会となります。

3.4 A coordinated effort for each RA's first major research

As a key class of the core curriculum in our program, the group project exercise takes place every Saturday. A lecture series on "my career path" by a variety of speakers with a wealth of experience is also scheduled on that day. The waterhole effect can clearly be observed when different values are exchanged and discussed. Therefore, all RAs get together with their highest priority in the program every Saturday. We have other activities as well, including progress meetings on Wednesday, summer and winter camps, and symposia; all events that can be remotely accessible using e-Learning Cloud system.

Giving priority to the first major with a flexible timing of course works enables RAs to take all other classes of the core curriculum and maintain their coordinated efforts for course works in both the first major research and leading program.

3.5 e-Learning cloud system (cloud-type remote education system)

Graduate schools of Keio University are located on different campuses, i.e., social sciences on Mita campus, medical sciences on Shinano-machi campus, science and technology on Yagami campuses, and governance and media on Shonan-Fujisawa campus.

In order to facilitate course works for the first and second major master's programs and to allow RAs to take a given class on a different campus, e-Learning Cloud System has been implemented to connect different campuses simultaneously.

4. Program curriculum

We have established the core curriculum of 24 lectures and exercises below in order to provide training for the RAs of this program to be leaders in a super mature society. Many lectures and

3.4 主専攻の研究との協調

　土曜日は、本プログラムが最も重要視しているグループプロジェクト演習が行われる日です。多様な経験を積んだ講師によるキャリアパス講演も開催されます。多様な価値観がぶつかり合う中で「水飲み場効果」も発揮されます。このため、本プログラムの土曜日の科目は最優先で履修する必要があります。また、水曜日の夕方開催されるプログレスミーティングや、夏・冬キャンプ、シンポジウム等の年間ビッグイベントも土曜日に準じて本プログラムが最優先となりますが、こちらは遠隔システムを介した参加も可能とします。

　一方、これ以外の共通科目の履修については、主専攻優先及び柔軟な履修タイミングを可能とすることで、主専攻との協調性を保ちます。

3.5 e-ラーニングクラウドシステム（クラウド型遠隔教育システム）の活用

　本学大学院は、文系は三田、医学系は信濃町、理工系は矢上、政策・メディア系は湘南藤沢というように複数キャンパスに分散しています。そこで、主専攻や副専攻の履修との協調のため、全員一拠点集合の土曜日を除いて、自キャンパスからe-ラーニングクラウドシステムにより授業に出席することが可能となっています。

4.　プログラム設置科目

　本プログラムで学ぶRA向けに、超成熟社会においてリーダーとして先導できるための素養を身に付けるため、下記24の共通科目を設置しま

exercises are from the Graduate School of Science and Technology, but we also have the cooperation of other graduate schools, such as Economics, from which the second majors can be selected.

Below is a summary of several aspects of the curriculum.

A List of Lectures and Exercises in 2015 for the PLGS "Science for Development of Super Mature Society"

Subjects	Faculty-in-Charge	Credits	The Graduate School that offers
Group Project Exercise1 ~4 (required)	Fumihiko Kannari Naoaki Yamanaka Yoshiko Ishioka	1	Science and Technology
Group Project Exercise5, 6(required)	Fumihiko Kannari Naoaki Yamanaka Yoshiko Ishioka	3	Science and Technology
Internship (required)	Kohei M. Itoh	2(spring) 2(fall)	Science and Technology
Environmental Economic Theory	Eiji Hosoda	2	Economics
Economics for Development of Super Mature Society	Jun Saito Yoshio Higuchi Kohei Komamura	2	Business and Commerce
Aging Society (recommended)	Atsushi Seike Yoshiyuki Sodekawa Kohei Komamura	2	Health Management, Media and Governance
Fundamentals of Epidemiology	Toru Takebayashi Makiko Nakano Sei Harada	2	Medicine
Policy Management(Human Security and International Development)	Michio Umegaki Kazunori Tanji	2	Media and Governance
Macroeconomic Developments and Economic Policy in Japan	Jun Saito	2	Science and Technology
Practical Intellectual Property Management 1,2	Kenichi Hatori	2	Science and Technology
Conference Communication	Yuuki Yonekura	2	Science and Technology
Introduction to Policy Recommendation Ⅰ, Ⅱ	Hiroshi Nagano	2	Science and Technology

した。設置研究科は、理工学が多いですが、経済学等、副専攻選択可能な研究科にも協力して貰っています。

　本科目のうちの、いくつかについて、概要を以下に紹介します。

Communication Skill 1(recommended)	Tsutomu Miyake	2	Science and Technology
Communication Skill 2(recommended)	Tsutomu Miyake	2	Science and Technology
Global Startup (recommendation)	Tsutomu Miyake	2	Science and Technology
Academic Technical Writing	Tsutomu Miyake	2	Science and Technology
Distance Operation	Kouhei Ohnishi Sota Shimizu	2	Science and Technology
Analysis and Design of Time and Space	Masayasu Yamaguchi Davisi Boontharm	2	Science and Technology

4.1 Group Project Exercises 1 – 6 (Graduate School of Science and Technology)

This course is the most important in the core curriculum; it is the only course work that will continue throughout the five-year MMD system. The mentors, mostly a manager (or equivalent) or higher-ranked official from renowned Japanese industries and/or a local government body, provide RAs with issues in industries and governments every Saturday. In a small group of RAs with a mentor, actual issues of a society will be provided that will allow the RAs to brush up their problem-identifying skills and planning and problem-solving abilities. Results of the exercise will be reflected as RAs' policy proposals and/or a long-term strategy of industries.

4.2 Internship and Study Abroad (Graduate School of Science and Technology)

RAs will be provided with the opportunity of internships during master's degree programs and to study abroad during doctoral degree programs. As a foreigner in different working and cultural environments, RAs will develop and cultivate their independency, cooperative attitude, and global awareness during their one-month internship. In their study abroad, RAs will have a chance to deepen their major research expertise with a sub-supervisor(s).

4.1 グループプロジェクト演習1～6（理工学研究科設置）

本プログラムが最も重視する科目であり、博士修了までの5年間に亘って履修します。日本を代表する企業や行政体等の部長クラスが、RAに対する指導者（メンター）となって毎週土曜日に来塾し、産業界や社会の生の課題をRAと共に掘り下げます。少人数にグループ分けされたRAは、メンターの指導の下で社会の生の課題を知り、問題発見能力や企画力・問題解決力を磨きます。その結果は政策／企業長期戦略提言に繋げます。多様な業界の社会人との円滑なコミュニケーションを学ぶ場でもあります。

4.2 学外特別研修（理工学研究科設置）

修士課程における海外インターンシップ派遣と博士課程における短期留学の2種類を用意しています。海外インターンシップでは、1カ月程度自分以外は外国人という異文化環境の中で就労体験をすることで自立心、協調性、国際感覚を身に付けます。短期留学では、海外の大学等に滞在し、副指導教員の下、自分の主専攻の研究を深化させる機会となります。（英語で開講）

4.3 Economics for Development of Super Mature Society (Graduate Schools of Economics and of Business and Commerce)

After providing an overview of the present state of the Japanese economy, which has reached the stage of a super mature society, this course will discuss ways to advance technological and institutional innovations that have the potential of resolving the problems and building a new era. For that end, a number of business areas will be taken up as case studies, and the issues to be addressed in those areas in terms of technology and institutional arrangement will be discussed from a long-term point of view.

4.4 Aging Society (Graduate Schools of Health Management and of Media and Governance)

An aging society seeks for improvement of health care, a review of the social security system, creation of a lifetime working platform, and better usage of spare-time. This course will examine issues for these agendas and plan a grand design(s). (Taught in English)
Practical Intellectual Property

4.5 Management 1, 2 (Graduate School of Science and Technology)

As a future leader who has been cultivated in the present program, the RA will be expected to embark on a global business as a generation of new industries to achieve QoL in an aging society with fewer children. Hence, a strategic use of global intellectual property rights system cannot be avoided during this process, and collaboration among industries, academia, and the government will be expected to play a key role in the process. By adopting a case study method with an introduction of the cases that have recently become a hot topic, the course will offer and allow students to gain practical knowledge of intellectual property rights and management.

4.3 超成熟社会発展の経済学（経済学／商学研究科設置）

　超成熟社会に突入した日本経済の現状を俯瞰した上で、それが直面する課題を克服し、新しい時代を切り開くための技術と制度のイノベーションについて議論します。その際、いくつかの産業分野をケーススタディとして取り上げ、そこにおける技術的・制度的な課題について長期的な観点から検討します。

4.4 高齢社会デザイン論（健康マネジメント／政策・メディア研究科設置）

　高齢社会ではヘルスケアの充実、社会保障制度の見直しとともに、生涯現役社会の創出や、長くなる余暇時間を活かしやすい社会が求められています。本科目はそのための課題を検討しそのグランドデザインを構想します。（英語で開講）

4.5 実践知財管理 1、2

　本プログラムで輩出を目指す将来のリーダーは、少子高齢化の中で、QoL を充実させる新しい産業の創出と、ビジネスの世界展開が期待されます。そのプロセスの中で、世界の知的財産権制度の戦略的利用が避けて通れません。また、その課程で、産学官連携に大きな役割が期待されています。これらをテーマに、近年話題となった事例を題材としたケーススタディ方式で、実践的な知識の修得を目指します。

4.6 Distance Operation (Graduate School of Science and Technology)

A key element to accomplish QoL in a super mature society will be a distance operation. In this course, RAs will participate in actual exercises of the da Vinci surgical system, haptics, and motion capture system and in a series of discussions. Through their experiences in the technologies and discussions, RAs will plan a system(s) of a new era by exploring the challenges for the commercialization of these technologies. (Taught in English)

4.7 Global Startup (Graduate School of Science and Technology)

Leaders in the drastically changing world will be expected to have both an understanding of the real world and the capability of discovering the hidden essence from
a broad perspective. In order to become such a leader, one of the best practices is to learn the spirit of entrepreneurship. By creating a mock venture company in this practical course, RAs can learn the fundamental way of thinking of successful entrepreneurs. RAs will also visit and talk with such entrepreneurs at an incubation center during the course.

4.8 Communication Skill 1 and 2 (Graduate School of Science and Technology)

To build the complete solution for global communication needs, this course will provide RAs with their individual English skills, including expressive and imaginary power, cross-cultural understanding skills, leadership skills, and problem-solving capability. All classes will be taught in a small group. (Taught in English)

4.6 Distance Operation（理工学研究科設置）

　超成熟社会において求められるQoLを実現する重要な要素に"Distance Operation"（遠隔操作）があげられます。そこで、現時点で最新の実用化システムであるdaVinciサージカルシステムやハプティクス、モーションキャプチャーシステム等を実際に操作し討論することで、その技術の実用化のための課題を探り、新時代のシステムを構想します。

4.7　グローバルスタートアップ（理工学研究科設置）

　次代のリーダーには、グローバルに世界情勢を把握し、幅広い視野で物事の本質を見抜く力を備えることが求められます。その獲得のための実践的な方法として、グローバルに成長するベンチャービジネスのスタートアップ（起業）をテーマにして、その思考方法を学び、現場見学と起業体験の演習を行います。

4.8　コミュニケーションスキル1、2（理工学研究科設置）

　グローバル環境への対応力を身に付けるため、英語での発想力と発信力、異文化理解力、リーダーシップ力および問題解決力を養うためのレッスンを少人数グループで展開します。（英語で開講）

5. Cultivating human resources through the collaboration with industry and government (Group project exercise): Brush up the ability of RAs to identify and solve problems

The group project exercise is the most important in the core curriculum of our program. Every Saturday, mentors, mostly a manager (or equivalent) or a higher-ranked official from renowned Japanese industries and/or a local government body, instruct RAs from a viewpoint different from the regular graduate education. In a small group of RAs with a mentor, the RAs will be provided with actual societal issues and brush up their ability to identify a problem(s) and to plan and solve it. Results of the exercises will be reflected as RAs' policy proposals and/or a long-term strategy for the industries.

For instance, in the group headed by mentor Shigeki Ishikawa, dispatched from IBM Japan (Ishikawa mentor seminar), the six students below from 1. to 6. are diligently applying themselves and gaining much inspiration and realization among themselves in the context of their diverse backgrounds.

1. Graduate School of Media and Governance D1 (Master's [Media and governance], Master's [Medicine])
2. Graduate School of Economics M1 (Second Master's degree) (Master's [Engineering])
3. Graduate School of Pharmacy M2 (Planning to continue to the Graduate School of Business and Commerce as second major)
4. Graduate School of Economics M2 (Planning to continue to the Graduate School of Medicine as second major)
5. Graduate School of Science and Technology M1 (DD study abroad from École Centrale Group*)
6. Graduate School of Medicine M1 (Second major is under consideration)
* DD study abroad allows students to study abroad based on

5. 産業界・行政体との密な連携による人材育成（グループプロジェクト演習）―問題発見能力・解決力を磨く―

　グループプロジェクト演習は、本プログラムが最も重視する科目です。日本を代表する企業や行政体等のキャリア経験豊かな方々（メンター）が、毎週土曜日に来塾し、これまでの大学院教育とは異なった視点でRAを指導します。メンター毎に少人数グループ分けされたRAは、メンターの指導の下で社会の生の課題を知り、今後我々が直面する超成熟社会を題材にして、問題発見能力や、その解決のための企画力・解決力を磨きます。その結果は、政策提言や企業長期戦略提言に繋げます。

　例えば、日本IBMから派遣いただいている石川繁樹メンターのグループ（石川メンターゼミ）においては、以下①～⑥の6人の学生が夫々の多様なバックグラウンドを背景に、切磋琢磨し、学生相互の間で多くの刺激と気付きを得ています。

① 政策・メディア研究科D1（修士（政策・メディア）、修士（医科学））
② 経済学研究科M1（副専攻）（修士（工学））
③ 薬学研究科M2（今後副専攻として商学研究科に進学予定）
④ 経済学研究科M2（今後副専攻として医学研究科に進学予定）
⑤ 理工学研究科M1（フランスのエコールサントラルグループからDD留学（注））
⑥ 医学研究科M1（副専攻は今後検討）
　（注）DD留学とは、本学と海外協定校との間で締結された「ダブルディグリープログラム」に基づいて留学するものである。一連のカリキュラムを修めると両校の修士号を取得することができます。

　本ゼミは、課題発見能力、俯瞰的な見方、課題解決力、リーダーに必要なコミュニケーション能力の育成を目標としています。

the "Double degree program" agreed between this school and affiliated schools overseas. After finishing the curriculum, it is possible to gain Master's degrees from both schools.

This seminar aims to nurture the ability to identify challenges, broad perspectives, problem-solving skills, and communication skills that are essential for leaders.

6. Cultivating a broad perspctive of view and vision through designing of three pillars

The greatest feature of our program is its focus on cultivating doctoral students with unprecedented knowledge and experience by achieving an integrated education of the arts and sciences with double majors and on making a collaborative effort among the university, industries, and the government. Although obtaining the second major master's degree along with the first major master's degree might be the major hurdle for students, we have established an educational system in which mentors from industries and government bodies guide and instruct students for the Group Project Exercise (GPE) every Saturday for five consecutive years. As the three pillars in our program, the first major and second majors and GPE ought to have some distances among their research projects. However, the three pillars are expected to make a great contribution to fostering students to build their own broad views and visions and ability for creative planning. In fact, we received high commendation that we have been cultivating doctoral students with unprecedented abilities when we exchanged opinions with human resources professionals from renowned companies in November 2014.

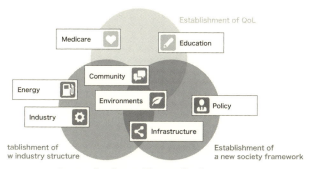

Issues for Super Mature Society

6. 三位一体設計による人間力形成（主専攻 / 副専攻 / グループプロジェクト演習）

　本プログラム最大の特色は、ダブルメジャー取得による本格的な文理融合の実現と、産業界・行政体との密な連携（産学官連携）による教育との効果的組み合わせにより、これまでにない学生を育成可能とした点にあります。主専攻と、その枠を大きく超えた副専攻の修士号を3年間で取得すること自体が高いハードルですが、それに加え、産業界・社会の視点で毎週土曜日に5年間継続してメンター指導するグループプロジェクト演習（GPE演習）という教育環境を整備しました。この主専攻、副専攻およびGPE演習を三位一体として構成し、その相互の研究主題を所定の距離感 d1、d2、d3 に置くことを課すことで、総合的俯瞰力や独創的企画力の形成に大きな貢献が期待されます。実際に、2014年11月に行なった5社以上の大企業人事担当者との意見交換において、これまでに無い人材が育っているとの高い評価を受けました。

7. Diverse activities that increase motivation (Overseas dispatch, summer/winter camps, etc.)

Key activities in our program consist of ones that are part of the core curriculum and others that are outside the core curriculum. As part of the core curriculum, we have presentations by RAs (as their group project exercise) and field works. Outside the core curriculum, we have the following activities: 1) progress meetings where RAs make a presentation (in English) on their major research to RAs with different backgrounds; 2) a series of career path lectures to enrich RAs' future perspective; 3) summer and winter camps where RAs, faculty members with different fields of expertise, and mentors exchange ideas; 4) global activities, including internships abroad and international workshops; 5) a symposium where yearly activities of the program are presented publicly; 6) a Forum of Program for Leading Graduate Schools, where all leading programs in Japan gather and exchange activities; and 7) various other activities. We will introduce the major activities below.

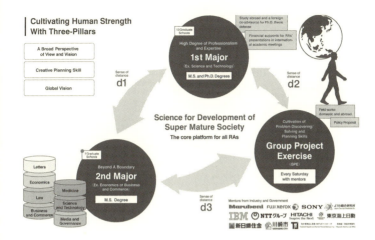

7. モチベーションを高める多様な活動（海外派遣、夏・冬キャンプ、e.t.c.）

　本プログラムの活動は、授業の一環で行われるものと、授業とは別に行われるものに分けられます。授業の一環では、グループプロジェクト演習の成果発表会やフィールドワーク等があります。一方、授業とは別に、主専攻の研究成果を異分野のRAに対して英語で発表するプログレスミーティング、自分の人生を2倍も3倍も豊かにし得るキャリアパス講演、泊まり込みで多様な分野の教員やメンターと討論できる夏・冬キャンプ、海外インターンシップ派遣や海外ワークショップに参加するグローバル活動、1年間の活動成果を広く社会に発信するためのシンポジウムや合同フォーラムへの参加等その他多様な活動があります。以下、主な活動を紹介します。

7.1 Progress Meetings

At a progress meeting, RAs periodically present (in English) on the progress of their first major studies (once during the spring and once during the fall semester). In addition to receiving guidance from an advisor for their majors, the presenters are guided in their research to enhance its quality by discussing multiple viewpoints with RAs in other fields, program committee members, and project professors.

7.2 Career Path Lectures

To help RAs design their career path, a rare but important opportunity is provided. They are given the opportunity to listen to a series of career path lectures that are given by experts with a diverse experiences and values. Each lecture might include the lecturer sharing his/her hardships in life, a turning point and/or an important decision, and a triumph. This will help RAs to design their career path in the future. By fully utilizing networks and/or connections that Keio University has established, a series of career path lectures will take place in the 5th period of course works on Saturday during the fall.

藤崎一郎氏
(元アメリカ合衆国 駐箚特命全権大使)
Ichiro Fujisaki
Former Japanese Ambassador to
the United States of America

國尾武光氏
(日本電気㈱執行役員)
Takemitsu Kunio
Senior Vice President, NEC
Corporation

7.1　プログレスミーティング

　プログレスミーティングは、RA が自身の研究の進捗状況を定期的に英語で報告する会議です（春学期と秋学期に全 RA が各1回発表）。発表者は、専門分野の指導教員からの指導に加えて、異分野の RA、プログラム担当教員、特任教員との多角的観点からの議論を通じて、研究の方向性や質を高めることができます。

7.2　キャリアパス講演

　RA が将来のキャリアパスを設計する上で、多様な経験や価値観を有した有識者から、人生の岐路と決断、挫折からのリカバリー等の話を聞くことは大変有益です。自らの人生を、2倍にも3倍にも豊かにデザインすることが期待されます。慶應義塾の人脈をフルに活かして、主に土曜日5限に開催されます。

7.3 Global Activities

At the internship in SanFrancisco

In our program, special trainings have been devised to help RAs to develop their views and visions and innovative planning ability, along with their major expertise. The trainings included will be four-week internships abroad during their master's programs (working experience in a foreign company, NPO, or organizations) and a half-year research study abroad during their doctoral programs (receiving research guidance by foreign sub-supervisors). Furthermore, field works abroad for their group project exercise and their presentations in international academic scientific meetings and workshops will all be considered as important global activities to exchange and discuss many issues and to establish a network with foreign experts.

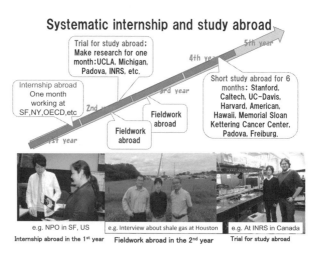

7.3 グローバル活動

本プログラムでは、共通科目のうち必修科目の一つとして、学外特別研修を設けています。修士課程において海外インターンシップ派遣（4週間程度、異文化の中で就労体験）、博士課程において短期留学派遣（半年程度、主専攻の研究について副指導を受ける）を行うことで、骨太の主専攻の上に、俯瞰力や独創的な企画力を身に付けることが期待されます。

このほか、グループプロジェクト演習に関連した海外フィールドワークや、主専攻や副専攻での海外学会発表や海外ワークショップにおいて、海外の専門家と討論し、ネットワークを構築することも、重要なグローバル活動と考えています。

これらの海外派遣は、下記のように、5年一貫の教育プログラムの中で、1～4年目に計画的に配置されます。

下記は、4年目に派遣される短期留学の事例です。研究成果は博士論文の重要な要素になります。また、博士学位審査において、本留学中に指導を受けた指導教員に副査をお願いすることにより、グローバルに質担保された学位の取得に繋がります。この留学で形成された人的ネットワー

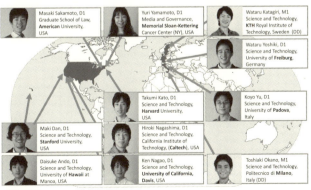

The Universities where RAs Study Abroad in 2015

These global dispatches are distributed strategically between years one and four during the five-year educational program.

Below are examples of short-term study abroad sessions that students attend in their fourth year. Research results will be important factors of the doctoral dissertation. In addition, by asking the mentor faculty who advised the RA during this study abroad to act as the associate examiner, the RA will be able to obtain a degree that has been internationally certified. The human network and connections made through this study abroad may develop and lead to stronger collaboration on the university level.

7.4 Symposium

A symposium is held at the end of each FY to conduct yearly activities and discuss the progress and challenges in our program. At the end of the 2014 FY, an international symposium—"Specialist vs. Generalist,"—was held in which a discussion took place between our RAs and students from École Centrale de Nantes (ECN), France. Keio University and ECN have had a double degree joint program. In addition, RAs have organized an RA forum—"The Future Japan beyond the Super Mature Society,"—and introduced the activities in our program.

7.5 Camps

Students are given various opportunities to make their presentations in English on their research findings or on assigned themes. In addition to progress meetings held during each semester and RA report sessions at the end of each semester, camps are held twice a year during the spring and winter semesters.

クが発展して、大学レベルでの協力の深化に繋がることが期待されます。

7.4 シンポジウム

1年間の活動成果や進捗状況・課題を広く社会に発信するために、毎年度末にシンポジウムを開催しています。第1回は、2011年度末に三田キャンパスの北館ホールで、第2回は、2012年度末に三田キャンパスの東館ホールで開催しました。

2013年度末は、三田キャンパスの北館ホールで行いました。第2回からは、RAによるポスター発表を同時開催して、日頃のRAの活動成果を参加した方々に紹介し、質疑応答することで、水飲み場効果が得られる場ともなっています。

7.5 夏・冬キャンプ

学生達には研究の成果や与えられたテーマについて英語で発表するいくつかの場が提供されます。学期中に行われるプログレスミーティング、学期末のRA発表会、そして年2回、春学期と秋学期に行われるキャンプです。

Camps bring together advisors, mentors (department manager-level) from a wide variety of industry and government sectors who lead group projects every Saturday, program committee members, project professors, and experts with a broad spectrum of career paths. These participants stay overnight during the camp sessions and provide RAs with advice from multifarious standpoints. Through discussions with one another and with advisors, RAs are able to broaden their horizons and cultivate their ability to solve problems in a logical manner, while simultaneously gaining unprecedented insights. As a forum for interaction among faculty and experts in a wide range of fields and sectors, summer and winter camps play a highly significant role as a "water hole."*

* "Waterhole": A metaphor for a faculty environment in which RAs interact and share ideas with professors, representatives of industry and government bodies, and RAs from other majors, similar to a waterhole in an oasis of the savanna where a variety of animals gather.

8. e-Learning Cloud system connecting campuses

System classes and various activities of the Keio PLGS are carried out not only at our multiple campuses in Japan but also across a range of affiliated sites overseas. As a means of minimizing the effects of physical separation and time differences among these sites in Japan and throughout the world, the program constructed a

Activities at the Camp

　キャンプでは主専攻の指導教員、毎週土曜日に行われるグループプロジェクト演習の指導をしていただく多様な業界の産や官のメンター（部長クラス）の方々、本プログラム関係の専任教員や特任教員等、多様なキャリアパスを有した専門家が泊まり込みで参加し、学生に対して多角的なアドバイスを与えます。学生と教員が互いに討論することで、学生は幅広い視野を持ち、論理的に物事を解決する力を養うとともに、新たな気づきが得られる場となっています。このように、多種多様な人々が泊まり込みで集うことから、夏・冬のキャンプは「水飲み場」（注）として大きな役割を果たしています。

(注)「水飲み場」：サバンナのオアシスにさまざまな動物が集まることで、歴史的に様々な種が発展したことに例えて、多様な分野の教授陣や産学官の経験豊富な有識者、主専攻を異にする学生が集うファカルティ環境。

8. 他キャンパスを繋ぐe-ラーニングクラウドシステム

　当リーディング大学院の授業と諸活動は、国内の複数のキャンパスはもとより、海外の連携拠点にも跨って実施されます。そこで、国内外の拠点間の物理的な距離の隔たりや時差の影響を最小限に抑えるための手段として、新しい教育クラウドシステム（通称：e-ラーニングクラウドシステム）

new educational cloud computing system—known as the e-Learning Cloud System—at all major campuses. The main services offered by this system are as follows: (1) remote lectures and meetings that make participants feel close and connected, (2) a lecture archive (live or streamed on demand), (3) e-learning English study tools, (4) sharing of academic and research materials, and other services. The system enables users to access these services flexibly and securely from off-campus locations throughout Japan and the world using laptop computers, tablets, or other devices. The e-Learning Cloud System became functional with lectures streamed remotely between the Hiyoshi and Shonan Fujisawa campuses during the spring 2012 semester. Today, the system is an indispensable part of a wide range of operations, including regularly scheduled lectures, progress meetings, and RA report sessions.

を構築しました。

このシステムが提供する主なサービスは、以下の通りです。①高臨場感遠隔講義／会議、②講義アーカイブ（ライブ／オンデマンド配信）、③e-ラーニング方式英語学習、④教育／研究資料共有、などです。また、これらのサービスに学外から安心・安全にアクセスできること、ノートパソコンやタブレットデバイスを用いて国内外のどこからでも柔軟にアクセスできること、などが主な特徴です。

システムの運用は、2012年度春学期の日吉～湘南藤沢キャンパス間の遠隔講義から始まり、今では日々の授業やプログレスミーティング、RA発表会などの諸活動に不可欠なものになっています。

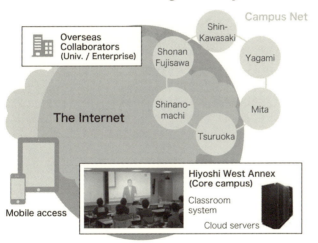

9. Members

9.1 Program Committee

In addition to the president of Keio University, program supervisor, and program coordinator, the committee consists of full-time faculty from the seven graduate schools who will participate in the joint-degree system as established by this university.

Atsushi Seike	President, Keio University
Akira Haseyama	Program Supervisor　Vice-President, Keio University
Fumihiko Kannari	Program Coordinator Professor, Graduate School of Science and Technology
Keiko Kurata	Professor, Graduate School of Letters
Koichi Toyama	Professor, Graduate School of Letters
Kohei Komamura	Professor, Graduate School of Economics
Koji Ishibashi	Professor, Graduate School of Economics
Hiroki Kawai	Professor, Graduate School of Economics
Kouji Mukawa	Professor, Graduate School of Law
Kinji Akashi	Professor, Graduate School of Law
Kazuaki Inoue	Professor, Graduate School of Law
Hitoshi Hayami	Professor, Graduate School of Business and Commerce
Atsushi Yashiro	Professor, Graduate School of Business and Commerce
Yuukou Kitagawa	Professor, Graduate School of Medicine
Hiroshi Itoh	Professor, Graduate School of Medicine
Toru Takebayashi	Professor, Graduate School of Medicine
Kazuo Tsubota	Professor, Graduate School of Medicine
Yoshiaki Toyama	Professor, Graduate School of Medicine
Masaru Mimura	Professor, Graduate School of Medicine
Masato Yasui	Professor, Graduate School of Medicine
Naohisa Yahagi	Professor, Graduate School of Medicine
Meigen Liu	Professor, Graduate School of Medicine
Kouhei Ohnishi	Professor, Graduate School of Science and Technology
Naoaki Yamanaka	Professor, Graduate School of Science and Technology
Kohei M. Itoh	Professor, Graduate School of Science and Technology
Tojiro Aoyama	Professor, Graduate School of Science and Technology
Hideharu Amano	Professor, Graduate School of Science and Technology

9. メンバー構成

9.1 プログラム担当者

　塾長、プログラム責任者およびプログラムコーディネーターに加え、本学が定めたジョイントディグリー制度に参加する7つの研究科の専任教員で構成されます。

清家　　篤	慶應義塾長
長谷山　彰	プログラム責任者　慶應義塾常任理事
神成　文彦	プログラムコーディネーター　理工学研究科 教授
倉田　敬子	文学研究科　教授
遠山　公一	文学研究科　教授
駒村　康平	経済学研究科　教授
石橋　孝次	経済学研究科　教授
河井　啓希	経済学研究科　教授
武川　幸嗣	法学研究科　教授
明石　欽司	法学研究科　教授
井上　一明	法学研究科　教授
早見　　均	商学研究科　教授
八代　充史	商学研究科　教授
北川　雄光	医学研究科　教授
伊藤　　裕	医学研究科　教授
武林　　亨	医学研究科　教授
坪田　一男	医学研究科　教授
戸山　芳昭	医学研究科　教授
三村　　將	医学研究科　教授
安井　正人	医学研究科　教授
矢作　直久	医学研究科　教授
里宇　明元	医学研究科　教授
大西　公平	理工学研究科　教授
山中　直明	理工学研究科　教授
伊藤　公平	理工学研究科　教授
青山藤詞郎	理工学研究科　教授

Hiroaki Imai	Professor, Graduate School of Science and Technology
Tadahiro Kuroda	Professor, Graduate School of Science and Technology
Yasuhiro Koike	Professor, Graduate School of Science and Technology
Kazunobu Toshima	Professor, Graduate School of Science and Technology
Midori Takayama	Professor, Faculty of Science and Technology
Takasumi Tanabe	Assoc. Prof., Graduate School of Science and Technology
Seiichiro Katsura	Assoc. Prof., Graduate School of Science and Technology
Shinichi Ueyama	Professor, Graduate School of Media and Governance
Jiro Kokuryo	Professor, Graduate School of Media and Governance
Hideyuki Tokuda	Professor, Graduate School of Media and Governance
Jun Murai	Professor, Graduate School of Media and Governance
Mitsuhiro Watanabe	Professor, Graduate School of Media and Governance
Miki Akiyama	Assoc. Prof., Graduate School of Media and Governance
Yasuhiro Naito	Assoc. Prof., Graduate School of Media and Governance
Toshiro Otani	Professor, Graduate School of Health Management

9.2 Mentors

These mentors are currently active in managerial positions at renowned Japanese companies and local governments. They will be given the position of part-time project professor at the Graduate School of Science and Technology and will supervise the mentor seminar every Saturday. They will also be involved in the employment of students by doubling as program committee members.

Shigeki Ishikawa	Business Development, IBM Research & Development -Japan, IBM Japan Ltd. Project Professor (Part-time), Keio University
Satoru Ueda	Senior Open Alliance Manager, Strategic Alliance Section, Sony Corporation Project Professor (part-time), Keio University
Yutaka Shimazaki	Corporate Officer General Manager, Executive Secretariat, Corporate Communications Dept. Marubeni Corporation Project Professor (Part-time), Keio University

天野　英晴	理工学研究科　教授
今井　宏明	理工学研究科　教授
黒田　忠広	理工学研究科　教授
小池　康博	理工学研究科　教授
戸嶋　一敦	理工学研究科　教授
高山　緑	理工学部　教授
田邉　孝純	理工学研究科　准教授
桂　誠一郎	理工学研究科　准教授
上山　信一	政策・メディア研究科　教授
國領　二郎	政策・メディア研究科　教授
徳田　英幸	政策・メディア研究科　教授
村井　純	政策・メディア研究科　教授
渡辺　光博	政策・メディア研究科　教授
秋山　美紀	政策・メディア研究科　准教授
内藤　泰宏	政策・メディア研究科　准教授
大谷　俊郎	健康マネジメント研究科　教授

(2015年4月)

9.2 メンター

　日本を代表する企業や自治体の現役部長クラスの方々により構成されます。本学理工学研究科の非常勤特任教授の職位を付与され、毎週土曜日のメンターゼミを主宰します。プログラム担当者も兼ねることで、学生の採用にも関与します。

石川　繁樹	日本アイ・ビー・エム株式会社　研究開発　ビジネス開発 慶應義塾大学理工学研究科　特任教授（非常勤）
上田　理	ソニー株式会社　設計品質技術2部　アライアンス戦略課 シニアオープンアライアンスマネージャー 慶應義塾大学理工学研究科　特任教授（非常勤）
島﨑　豊	丸紅株式会社　参与　秘書部長　兼　広報部長 慶應義塾大学理工学研究科　特任教授（非常勤）
高橋雄一郎	特許業務法人高橋・林アンドパートナーズ代表　弁護士 慶應義塾大学理工学研究科　特任教授（非常勤）

Yuichiro Takahashi	Senior Partner, Takahashi Hayashi and Partner Patent Attorneys Inc. Project Professor (Part-time), Keio University
Toru Yamasaki	Executive Research Principal, Research & Technlogy Group, Fuji Xerox Co., Ltd. Project Professor (Part-time), Keio University
Shoji Yamada	Director, Department of Self-Government Promotion, General Planning Bureau, City of Kawasaki Mentor, Keio University
Masayoshi Murase	General Manager, Head of Department, Personnel Dept., Research & Development, Nippon Steel & Sumitomo Metal Corporation Project Professor (Part-time), Keio University
Ryuzou Takahashi	Senior Fellow, Tokio Marine & Nichido Human Resources Academy Co., Ltd. Project Professor (Part-time), Keio University
Toshiyasu Himori	General Manager, Gunma Branch, Saitama Division, Nippon Telegraph and Telephone East Corporation Director, Gunma Branch, NTT EAST-KANSHINETSU Corporation Project Professor (Part-time), Keio University
Masashi Sawa	Director, Hitachi Institute of Technology, Hitachi, Ltd. Project Professor (Part-time), Keio University
Masataka Ota	Chief Consultant Consulting Department, Japan Tourism Marketing Co. Project Professor (Part-time), Keio University

9.3 Project Professors

These are project professors who have been employed for the development of this program. They will support the program operations, in addition to the core curriculum, and will double as program committee members.

Kenichi Hatori	Project Professor, Graduate School of Science and Technology
Tsutomu Miyake	Project Professor, Graduate School of Science and Technology
Jun Saito	Project Professor, Graduate School of Business and Commerce
Masayasu Yamaguchi	Project Professor, Graduate School of Science and Technology

山崎　徹	富士ゼロックス株式会社　研究技術開発本部研究主幹 慶應義塾大学理工学研究科　特任教授（非常勤）
山田　祥司	川崎市　総合企画局　自治推進部　部長 慶應義塾大学理工学研究科　メンター
村瀬　賢芳	新日鐵住金株式会社　技術開発本部　人事室長 慶應義塾大学理工学研究科　特任教授（非常勤）
髙橋　竜三	株式会社東京海上日動HRA　シニアフェロー 慶應義塾大学理工学研究科　特任教授（非常勤）
日森　敏泰	東日本電信電話株式会社　埼玉事業部　群馬支店長 株式会社NTT東日本―関信越　取締役　群馬支店長 慶應義塾大学理工学研究科　特任教授（非常勤）
沢　真司	株式会社日立製作所　日立総合技術研修所　所長 慶應義塾大学理工学研究科　特任教授（非常勤）
太田　正隆	株式会社JTB総合研究所　コンサルティング事業部　主席研究員 慶應義塾大学理工学研究科　特任教授（非常勤）

（2015年4月）

9.3　特任教員

本プログラム推進のために雇用された特任教員です。共通科目の担当のほか、プログラム運営をサポートします。プログラム担当者も兼ねています。

羽鳥　賢一	理工学研究科　特任教授
三宅　力	理工学研究科　特任教授
齋藤　潤	商学研究科　特任教授
山口　正泰	理工学研究科　特任教授
清水　創太	理工学研究科　特任准教授
石岡　良子	理工学研究科　特任助教
Peter Ventzek	理工学研究科　特任教授（非常勤） Tokyo Electron America, Inc.

Sota Shimizu	Project Associate Professor, Graduate School of Science and Technology
Ryoko Ishioka	Project Research Associate, Graduate School of Science and Technology
Peter Ventzek	Project Professor (Part-time), Graduate School of Science and Technology, Tokyo Electron America, Inc.
Davisi Boontharm	Project Associate Professor (Part-time), Graduate School of Science and Technology Associate Professor, Center for Global Discovery, Faculty of Foreign Studies, Sophia University

9.4 Board Council

Listed below are the members of the board who will provide advice from an intermediate standpoint between the university and industry/government. They will also support the dispatch of mentors.

Toshiaki Makabe	Vice-President, Board Council Chairman
Kaoru Kuzume	Corporate Auditor, Marubeni Corporation
Mitsunori Takeuchi	Senior Manager, Global Talent Management Department, Human Capital Group, Hitachi, Ltd.
Takeshi Hibiya	Audit & Supervisory Board Member, Fuji Xerox Co., Ltd.
Atsushi Miura	Deputy Mayor, City of Kawasaki
Hirotsune Satoh	Managing Executive Officer, Nippon Steel & Sumitomo Metal Corporation
Yoshihiko Nagasato	Counselor, Asahi Research Center Co., Ltd
Shun Kagata	Senior Manager, R&D Planning Group, Research and Development Planning Department Nippon Telegraph and Telephone Corporation
Akira Haseyama	Vice-President (Program Supervisor)
Fumihiko Kannari	Professor, Graduate School of Science and Technology (Program Coordinator)
Kouhei Ohnishi	Professor, Graduate School of Science and Technology (Previous Program Coordinator)
Kenichi Hatori	Project Professor, Graduate School of Science and Technology (Program Officer)

Davisi Boontharm	理工学研究科　特任准教授（非常勤） 上智大学　外国語学部

(2015 年 4 月)

9.4 ボード会議

大学と産業界との間に位置して、本プログラムに助言を与えます。また、メンターの派遣に対して支援をします。

真壁　利明	常任理事 ボード会議議長
葛目　薫	丸紅株式会社　監査役
竹内　光憲	株式会社日立製作所　人財統括本部 グローバルタレントマネジメント部長
日比谷　武	富士ゼロックス株式会社　常勤監査役
三浦　淳	川崎市 副市長
佐藤　博恒	新日鐵住金株式会社　常務執行役員
永里　善彦	株式会社旭リサーチセンター　相談役
加賀田　俊	日本電信電話株式会社　研究企画部門 R&D 推進　担当部長
長谷山　彰	常任理事（プログラム責任者）
神成　文彦	理工学研究科 教授（プログラムコーディネーター）
大西　公平	理工学研究科 教授（前プログラムコーディネーター）
羽鳥　賢一	理工学研究科 特任教授（プログラムオフィサー）

(2015 年 4 月)

Editorial Note

Toshiaki Makabe (Board Council Chairman, Keio Program for Leading Graduate School)

Having entered into the 21st century, we are all sensing that society has reached the point of transformation. Japan, in particular, has grown into a "super mature society," and it requires the construction of a new society with the capacity for sustainable development. At this time, we invited the presidents of five eminent universities that continue to produce highly skilled graduates, (i.e., the University of Tokyo, Oxford University, École Centrale Nantes, National University of Singapore, and Keio University), to the International Presidents' Forum. The forum was held on the afternoon of March 3, 2015, at the Mita Campus of Keio University, and it aimed at diverse discussions on how these institutions can build on their unique, historical foundations to nurture highly skilled human resources who could lead this transitional period and send them out to society. Chapter 1 of Part 1 described the structure and functions of the universities that participated in the discussions, and Chapter 2 included a direct transcription of the spirited discussion that followed regarding these functions.

Chapter 1 of Part 2 was taken from the foreword of a newsletter published by "Science for Development of Super Mature Society" of the Keio Program for Leading Graduate School, summarizing the hopes and requests expressed by individuals in various fields. Chapter 2 introduced the aims of Keio University regarding the Program for Leading Graduate School as well as the plans for realizing these goals. We hope that our efforts at Keio University can be used as an example for others.

We express our gratitude to those who participated in the Presidents' Forum and contributed to the foreword, and we would like to note that their titles, statements, and referential documents are of the time at which they were recorded.

編集後記

真壁利明（慶應義塾大学リーディング大学院プログラム　ボード会議議長）

　21世紀のいま、誰もが社会は変革期にあると感じています。特に、日本では超成熟社会に入り、新しい社会の構築とその持続的発展が求められています。この時期、高度大学院人材を輩出し続けている東京大学、オックスフォード大学、エコール　サントラル　ナント、シンガポール国立大学と慶應義塾大学が、それぞれ独特な歴史的基盤の上で、この変革期を担う高度人材をどのように育成し社会へ輩出しようとしているかなど、ダイバーシティーの高い議論を期待して、それぞれ5つの研究大学の学長をお招きし、今年3月3日の午後、慶應義塾大学の三田キャンパスで国際学長フォーラムを開催しました。講演頂いた各大学の構造や機能を第1部第1章に収録し、第2章では引き続き行われたこの機能についての熱い議論をそのまま載せさせていただきました。

　第2部第1章では、慶應義塾大学のリーディング大学院プログラム、「超成熟社会発展のサイエンス」が発行しているニュースレターの巻頭言を再録し、各界各氏からの期待と要望をまとめさせていただきました。第2章ではリーディング大学院プログラムに対する慶應義塾の意図と、これを実現する仕組みを紹介しています。慶應義塾の取り組みがご参考となればとの思いです。

　なお、学長フォーラムご参加の皆様、ならびに巻頭言をご執筆いただいた皆様の肩書、ご発言内容や資料は収録時点のものであることをお断りして、あらためて皆様に感謝申し上げます。

　終わりに、英文テープ起こしの段階から和文翻訳原稿が仕上がり出版に至るまで、羽鳥賢一教授（リーディング大学院プログラム）と、佐藤聖氏（慶應義塾大学出版会）の忍耐強いご協力なしでは出版の実現は難しかったことを付記し、両氏に心から御礼申し上げます。

Finally, we would like to acknowledge Professor Kenichi Hatori (Program for Leading Graduate School) and Mr. Takashi Sato (Keio University Press) for their unwavering patience and support. Without their support, from transcribing English recordings to finalizing the Japanese translation manuscripts and sending them to press, publication would have been difficult. We sincerely appreciate their efforts.

超成熟社会発展のサイエンス
　超成熟社会をリードするグローバル博士人材の育成

2015 年 12 月 15 日　初版第 1 刷発行

編者────慶應義塾大学博士課程教育リーディングプログラム
　　　　　「超成熟社会発展のサイエンス」
発行者───坂上　弘
発行所───慶應義塾大学出版会株式会社
　　　　　〒108-8346　東京都港区三田 2-19-30
　　　　　TEL〔編集部〕03-3451-0931
　　　　　　　〔営業部〕03-3451-3584〈ご注文〉
　　　　　　　〔　〃　〕03-3451-6926
　　　　　FAX〔営業部〕03-3451-3122
　　　　　振替　00190-8-155497
　　　　　http://www.keio-up.co.jp/
装丁────宮川なつみ
組版────ステラ
印刷・製本──中央精版印刷株式会社
カバー印刷──株式会社太平印刷社

©2015 Keio Program for Leading Graduate School "Science for Development of Super Mature Society"
　　Printed in Japan　　ISBN978-4-7664-2265-8